THIS COLORING BOOK BELONGS TO:

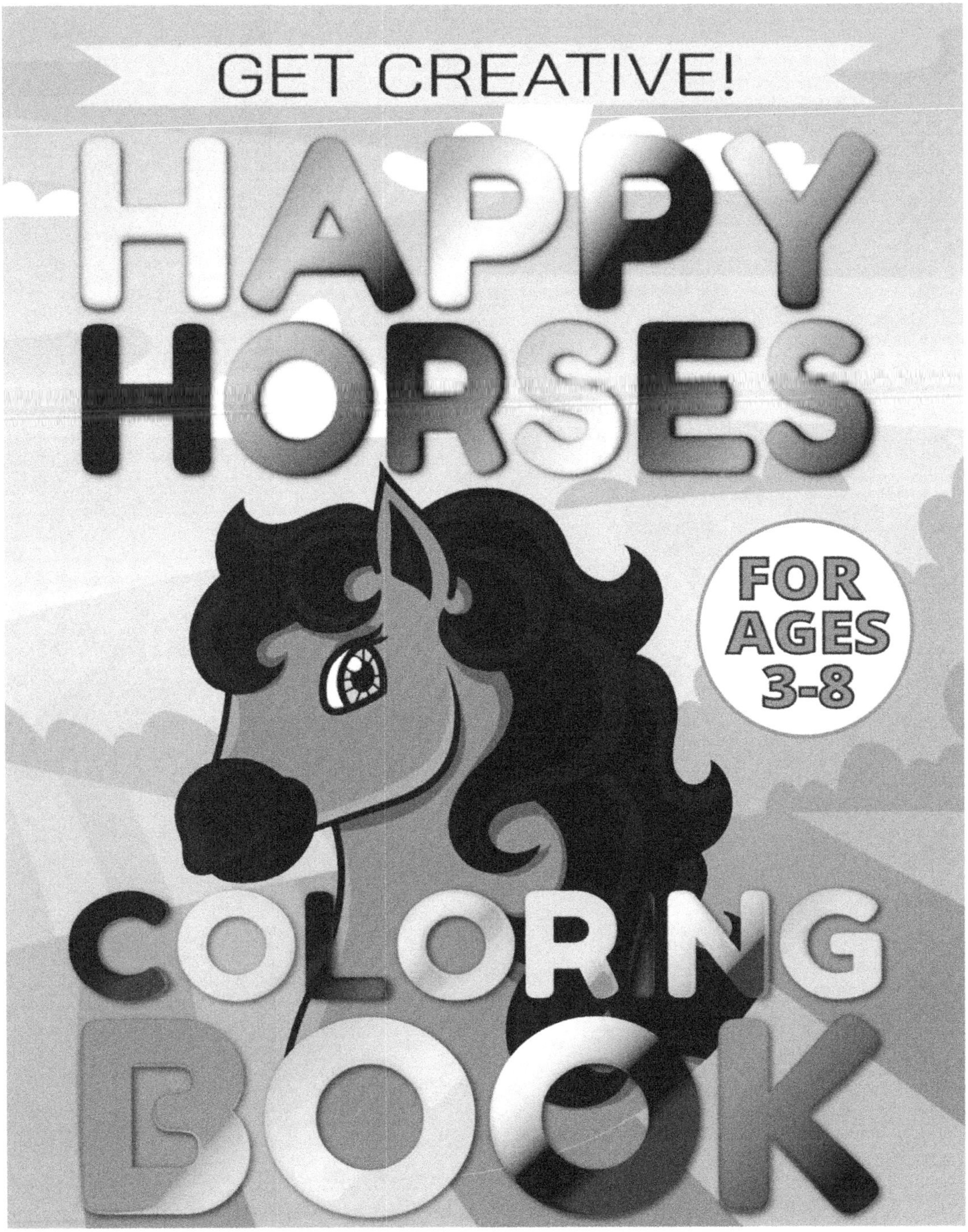

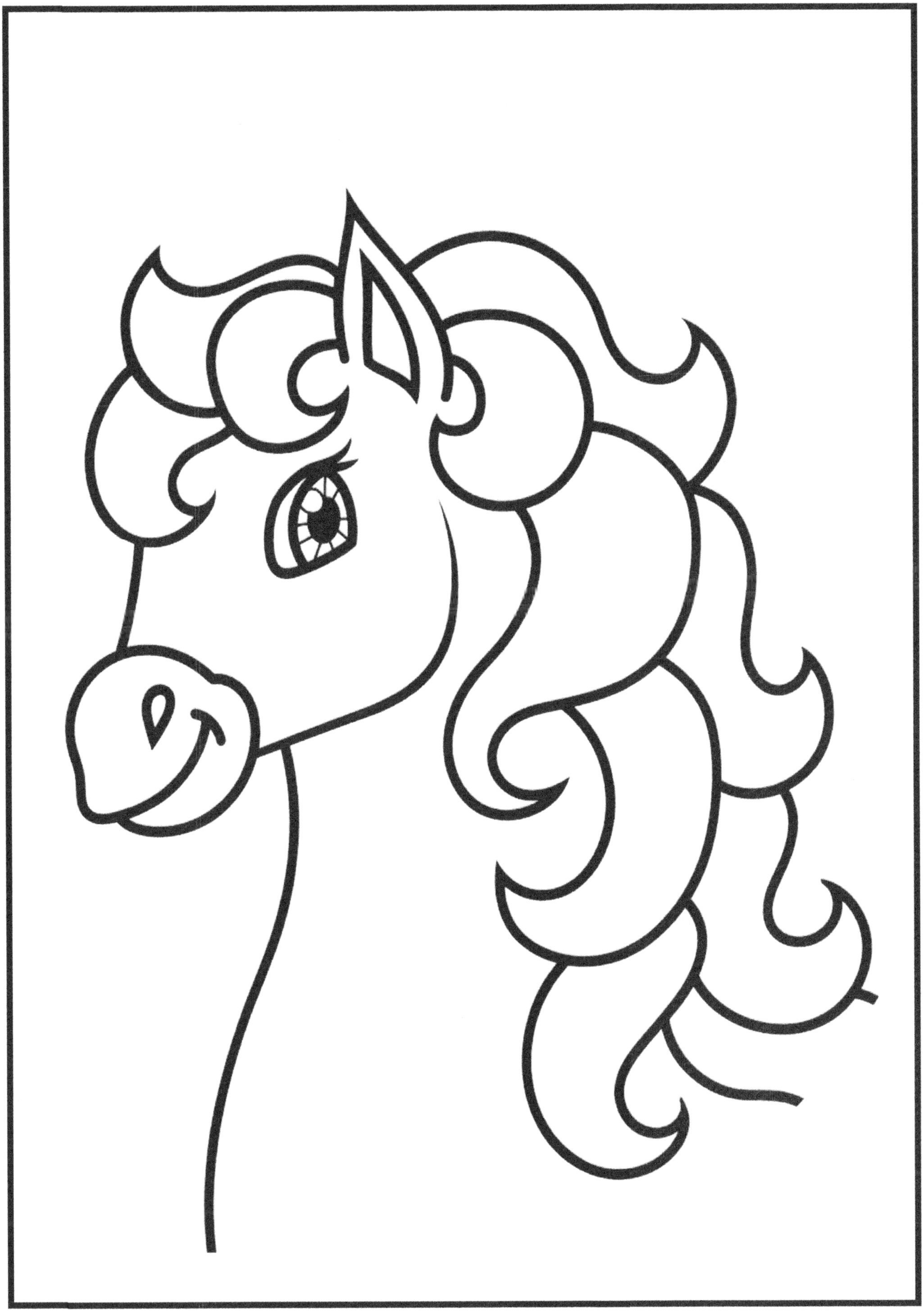

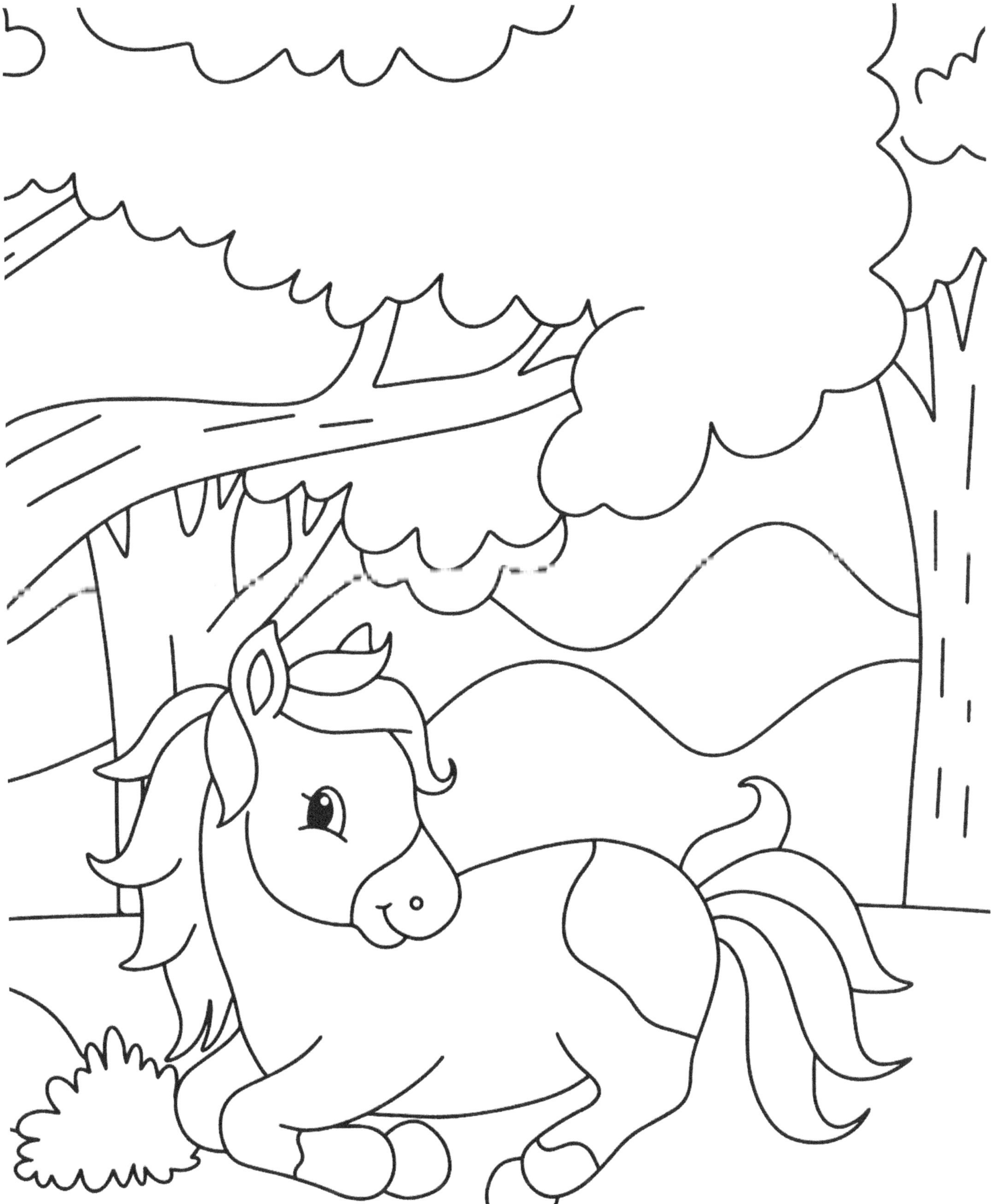

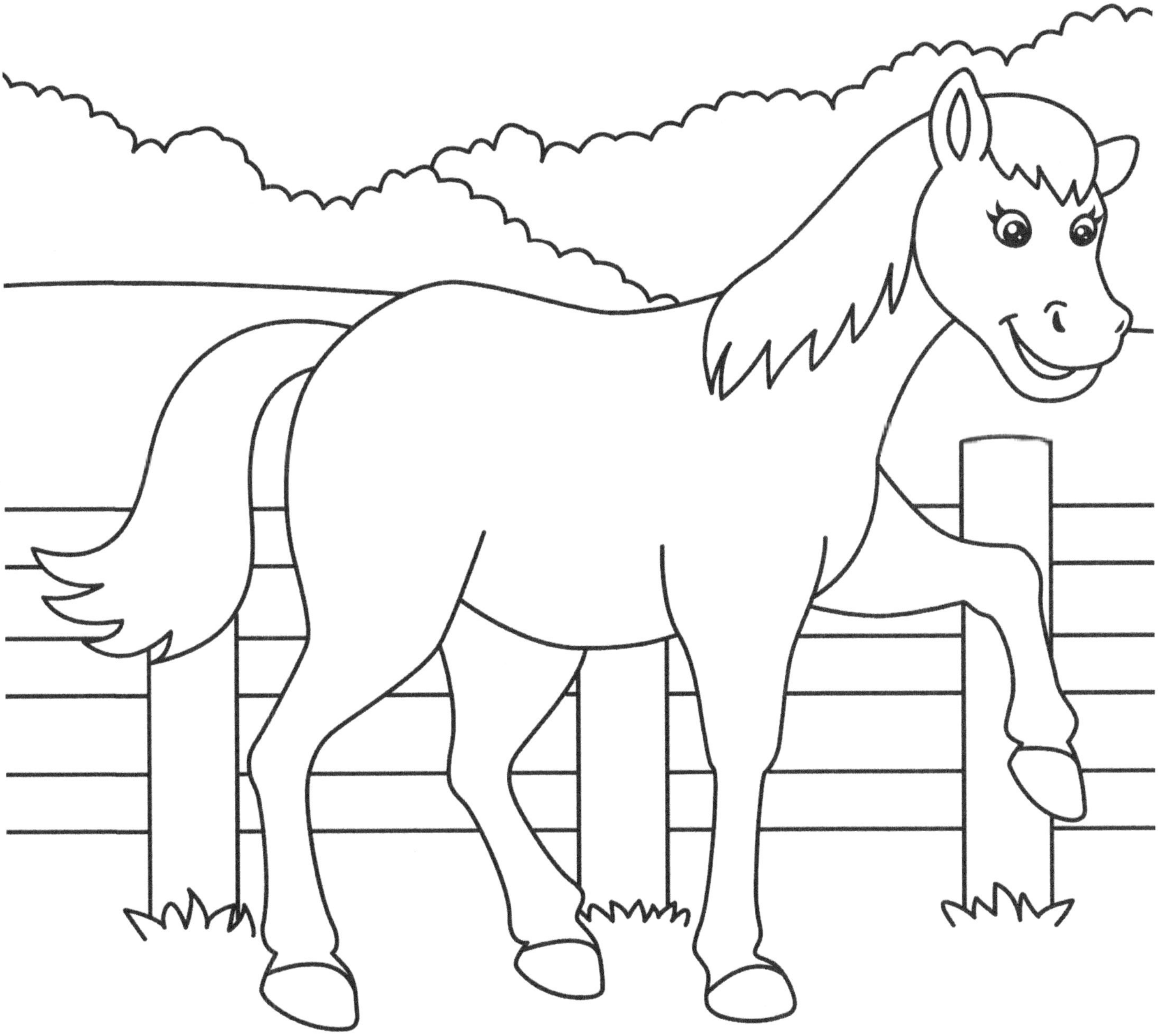

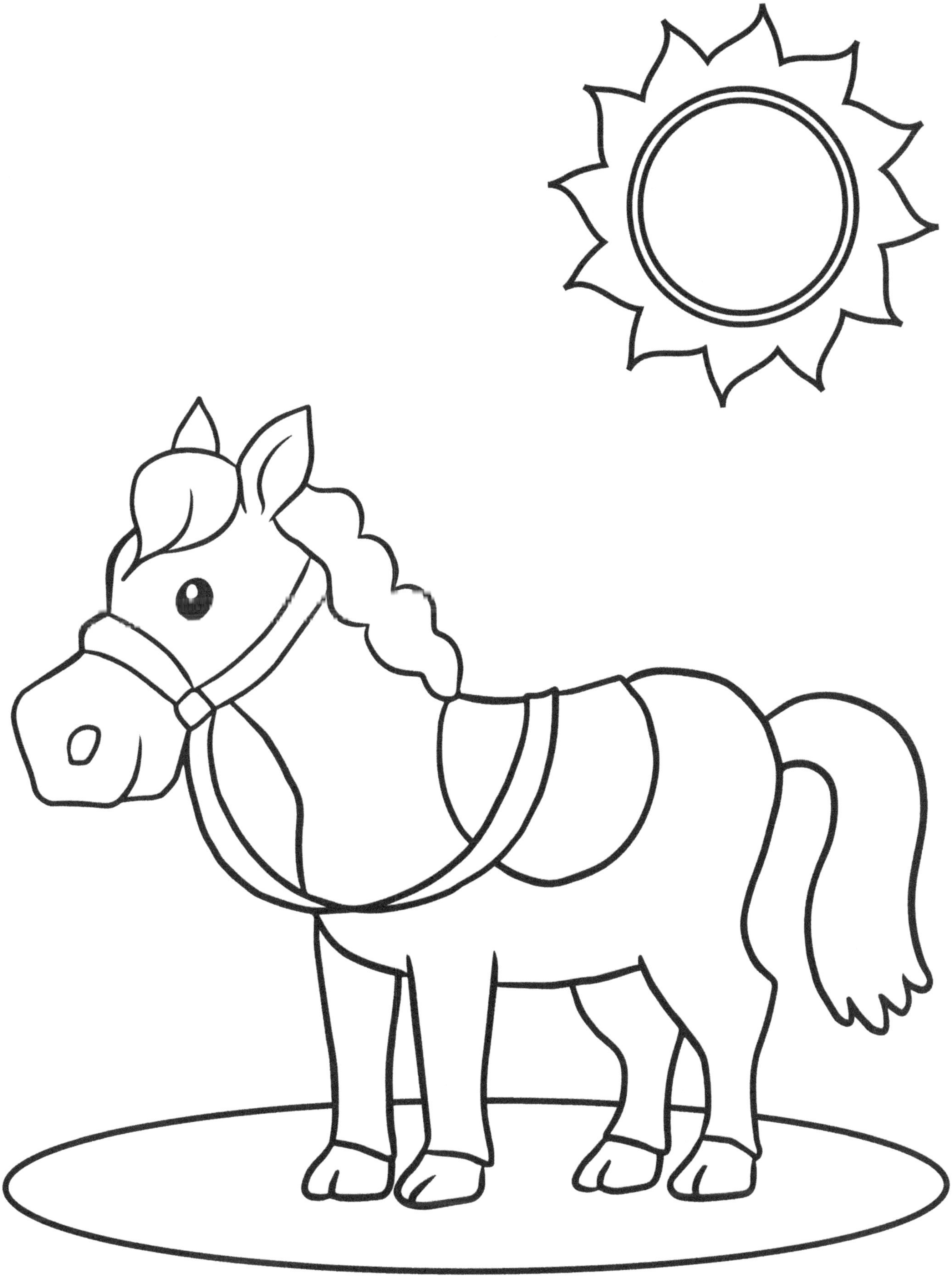

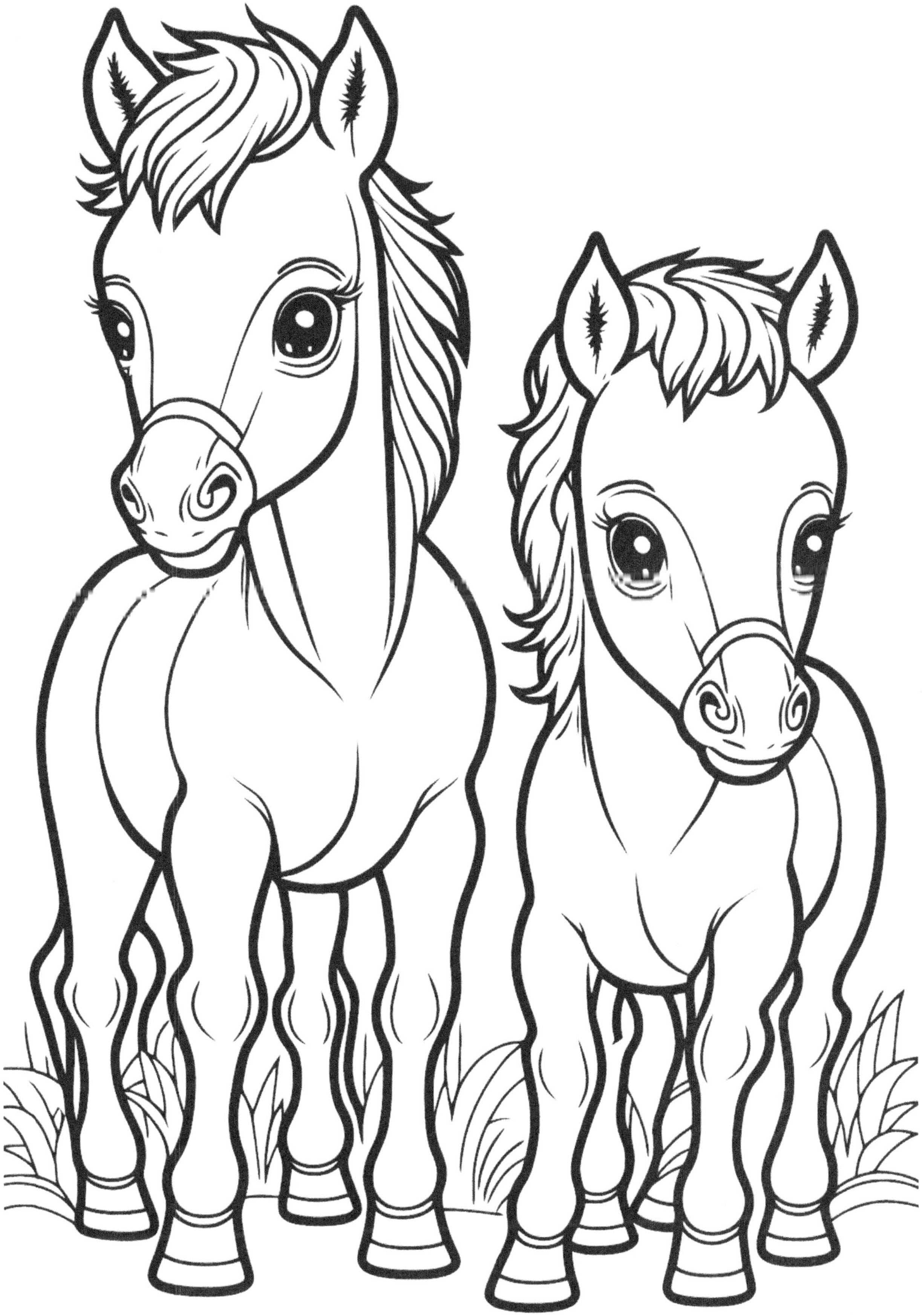

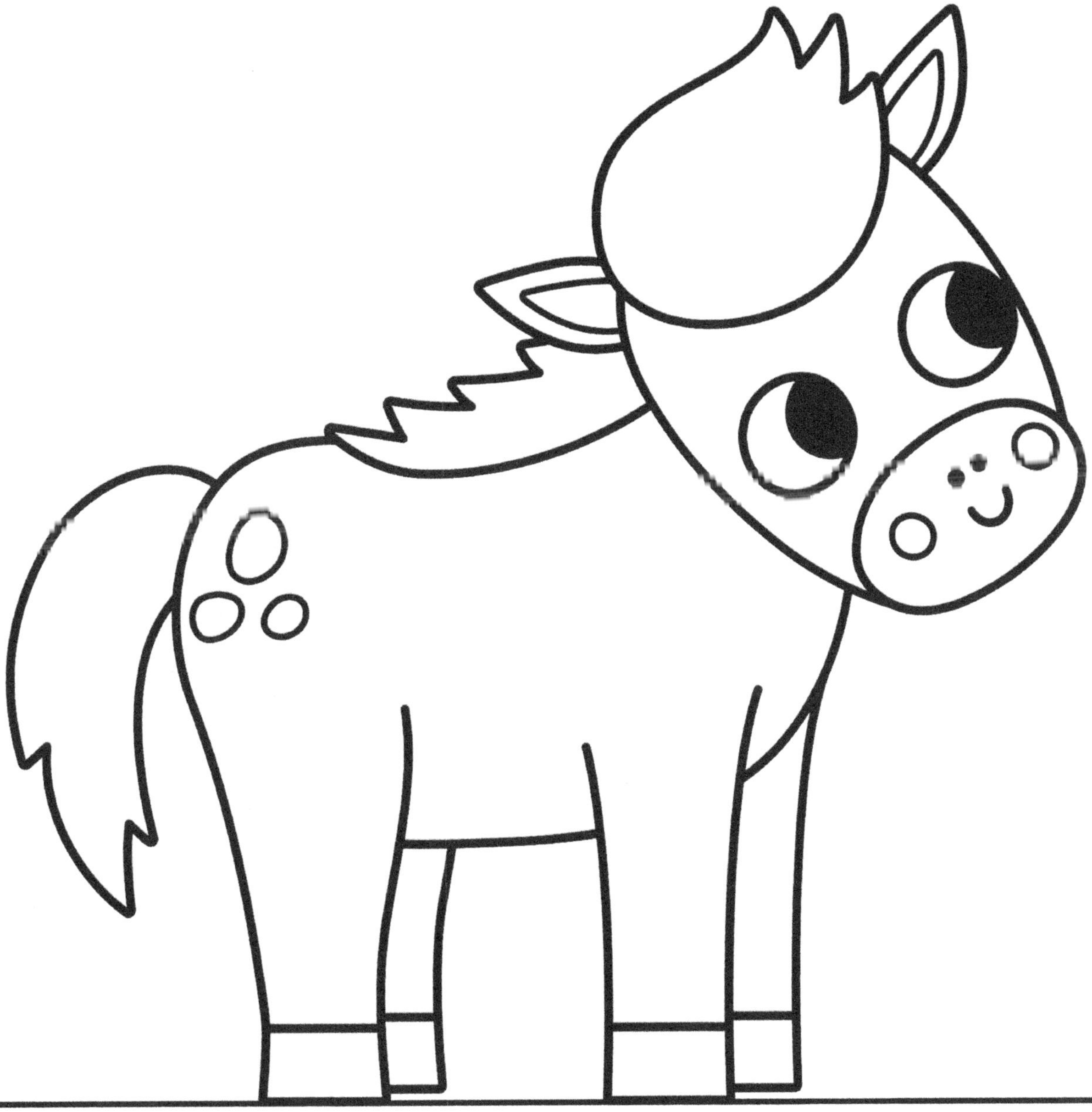

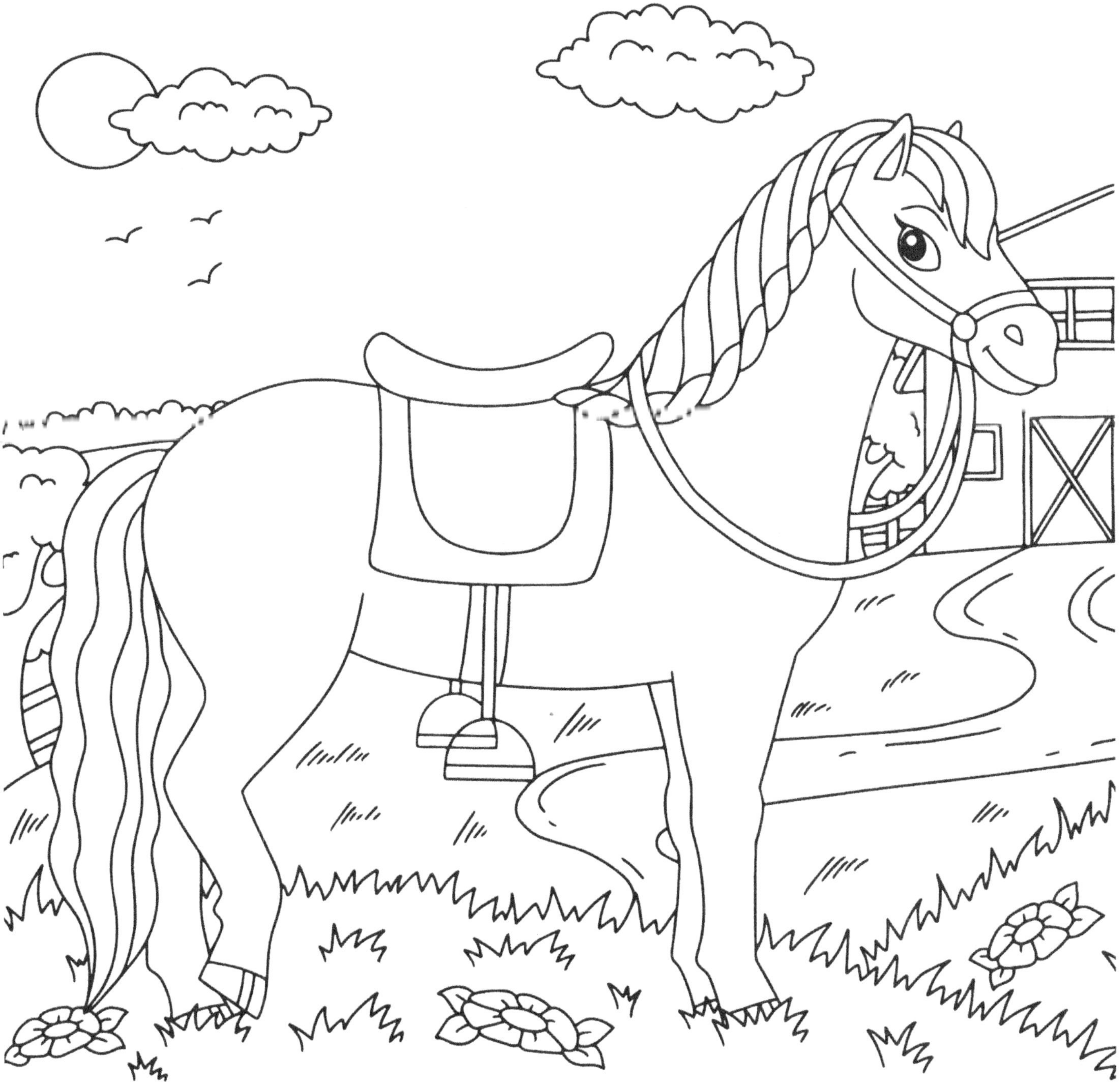

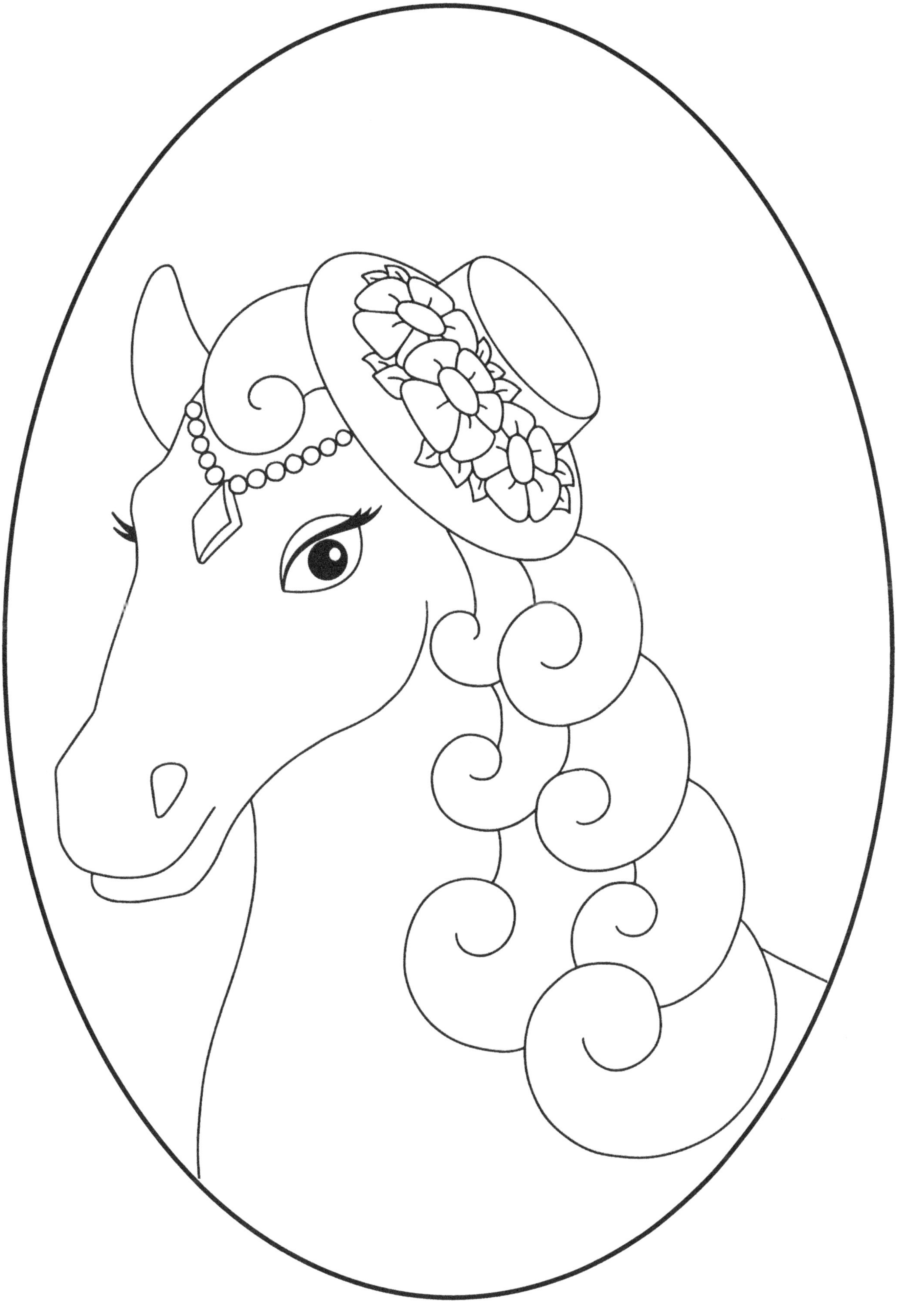

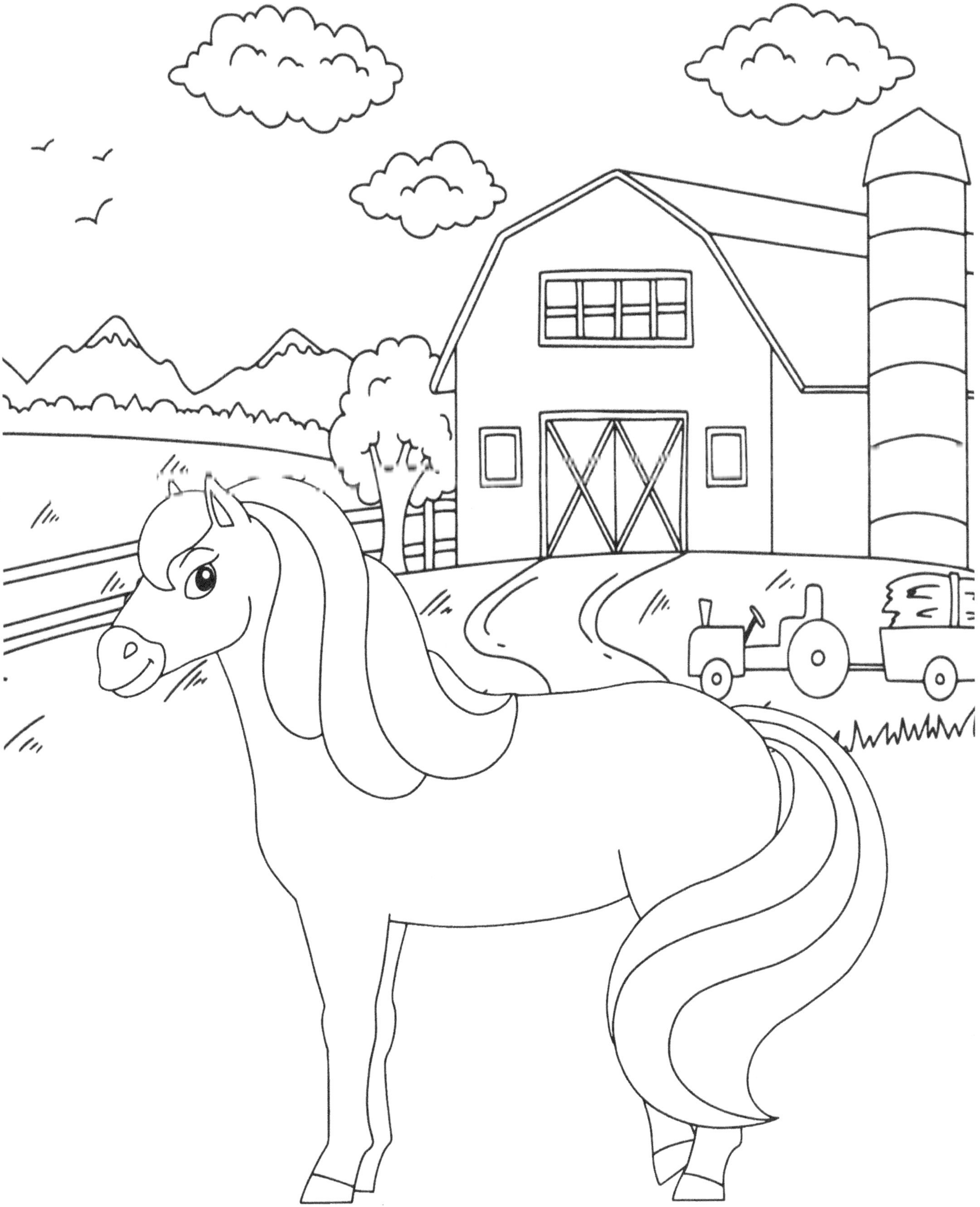

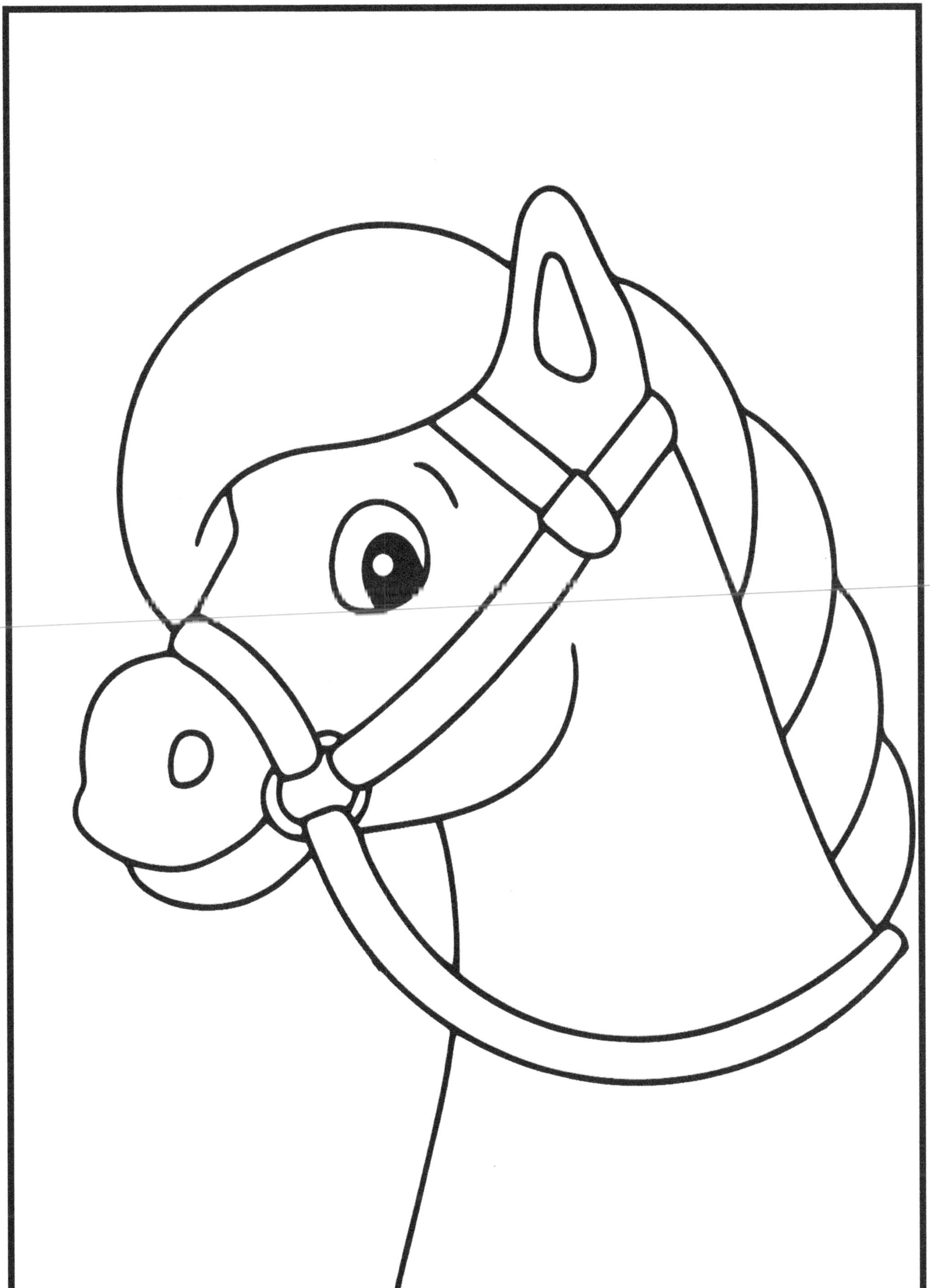

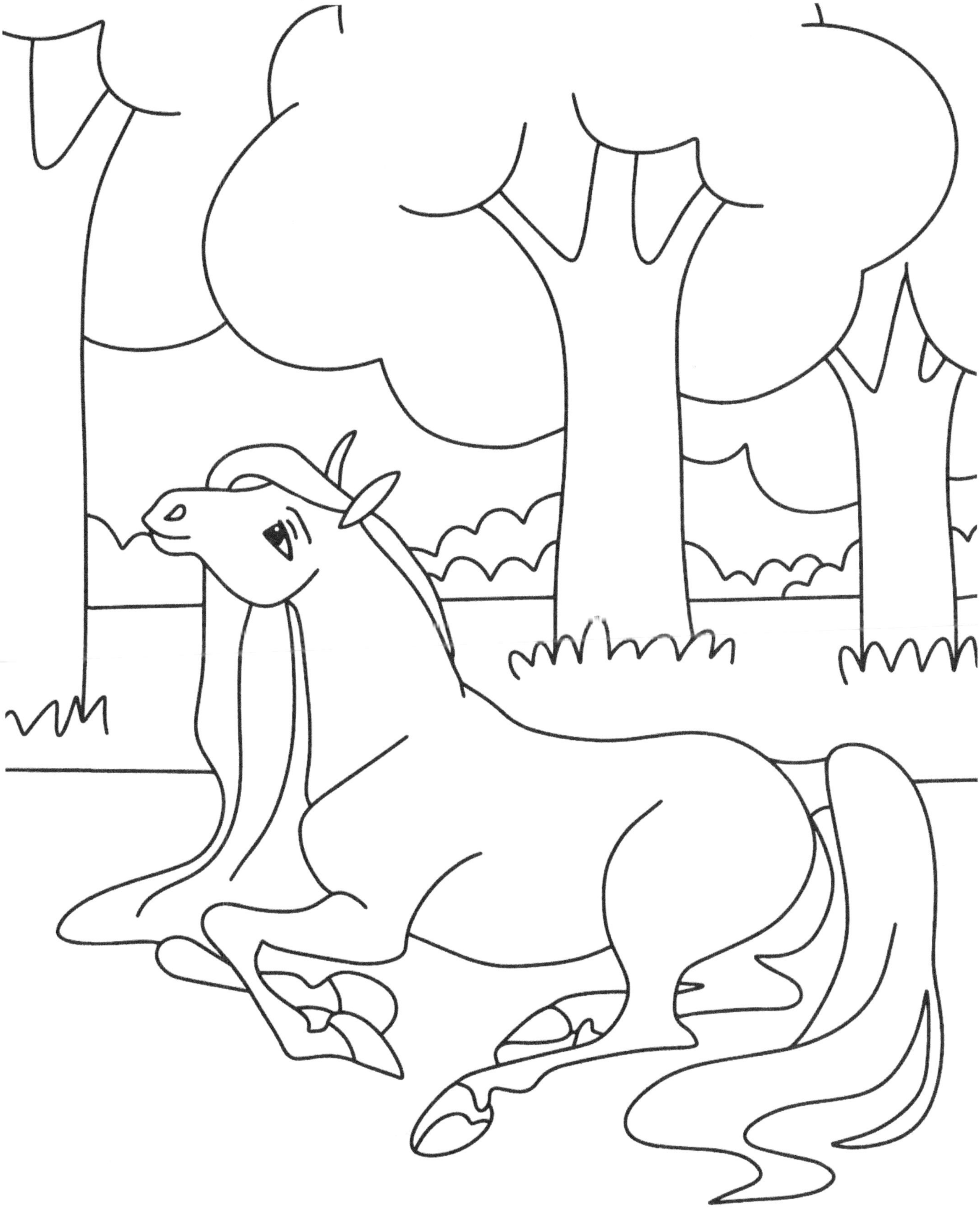

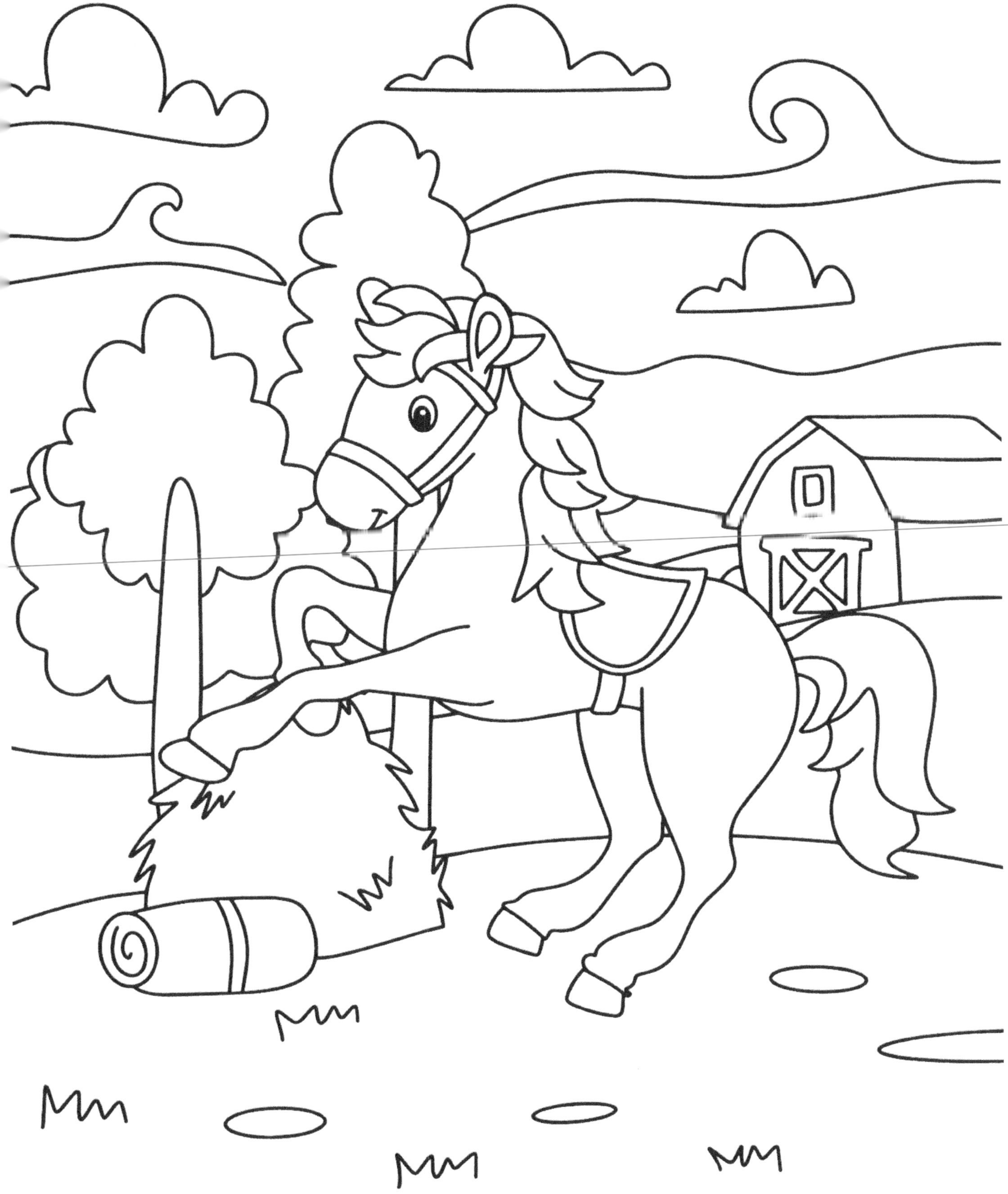

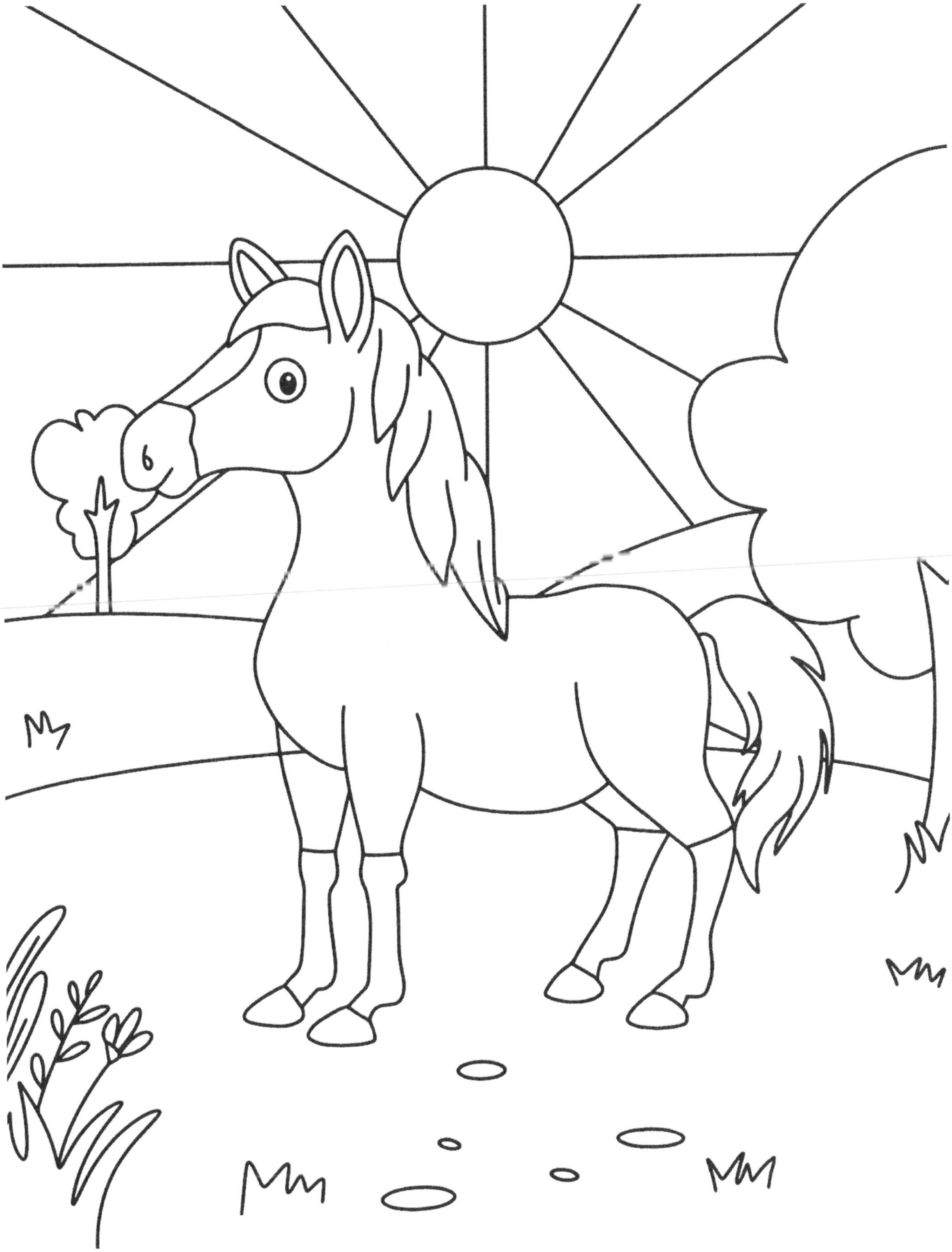

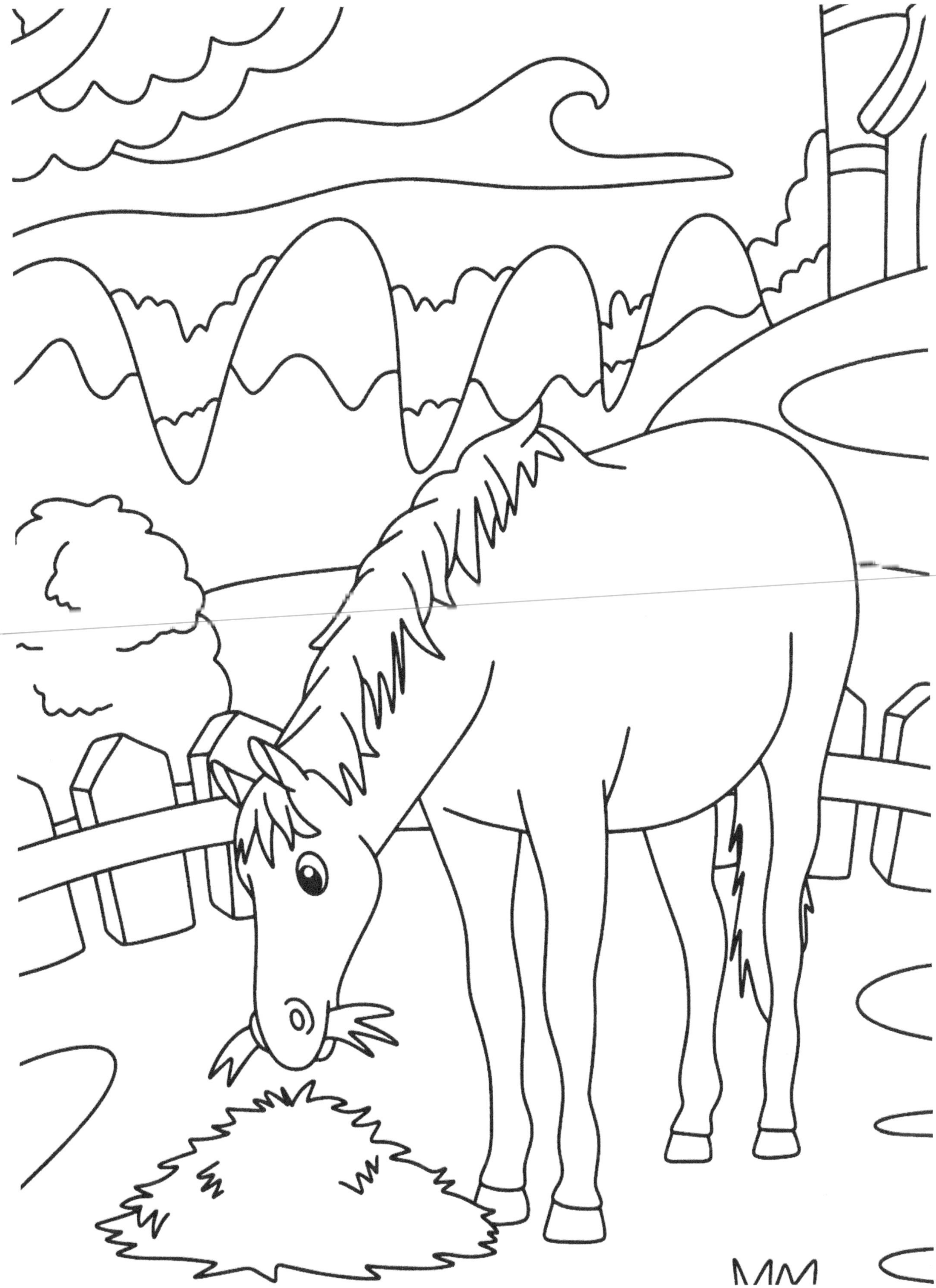

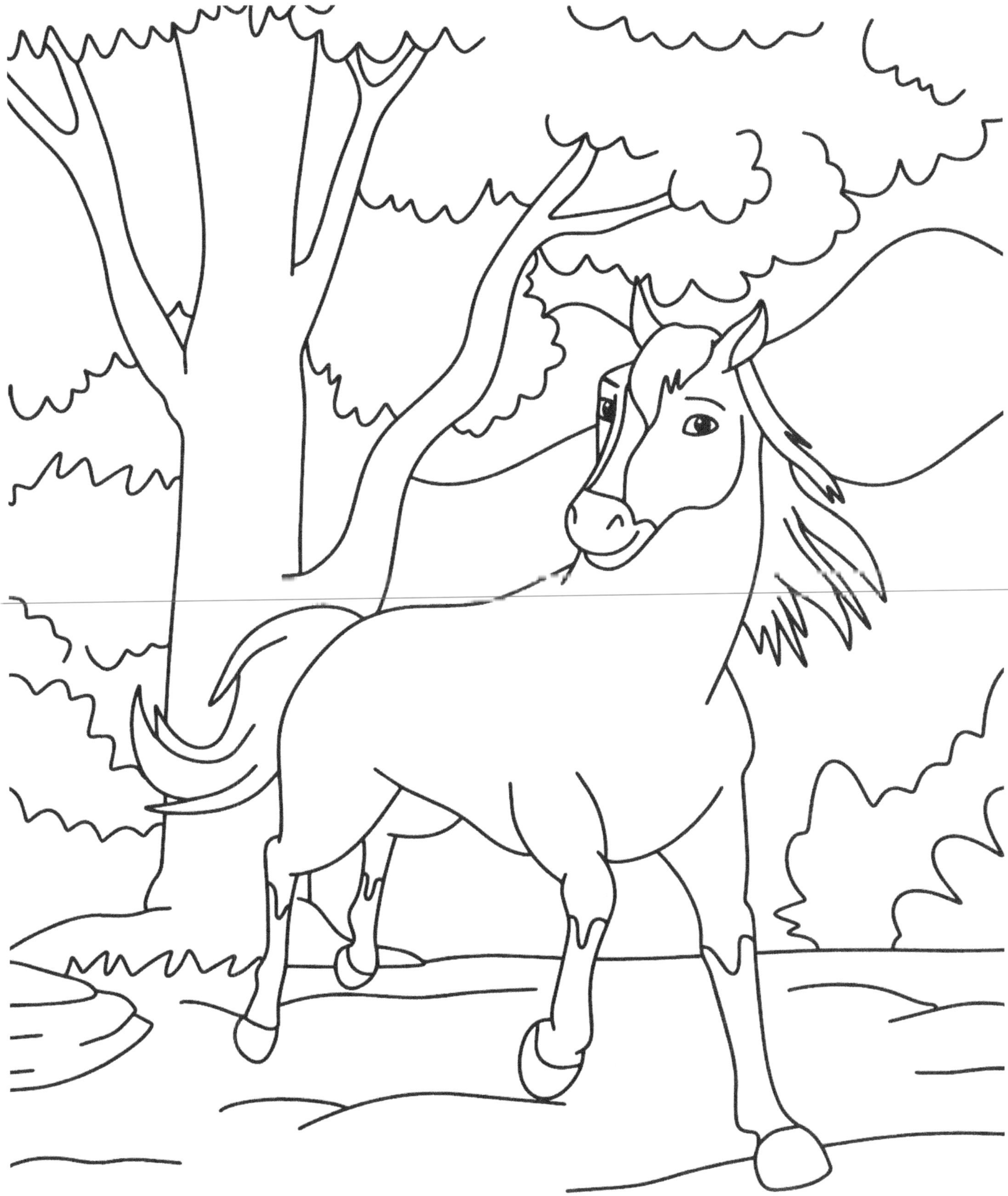

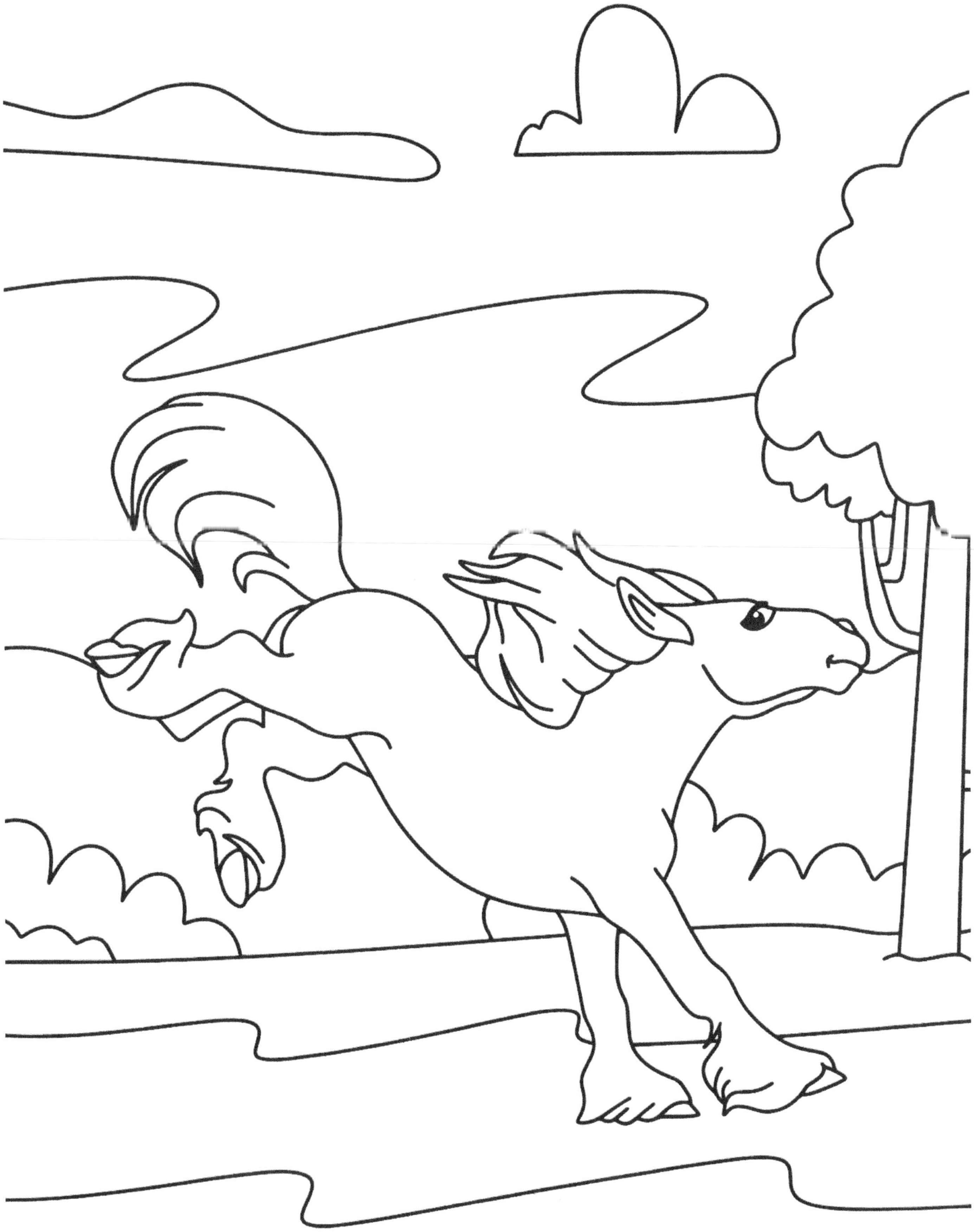

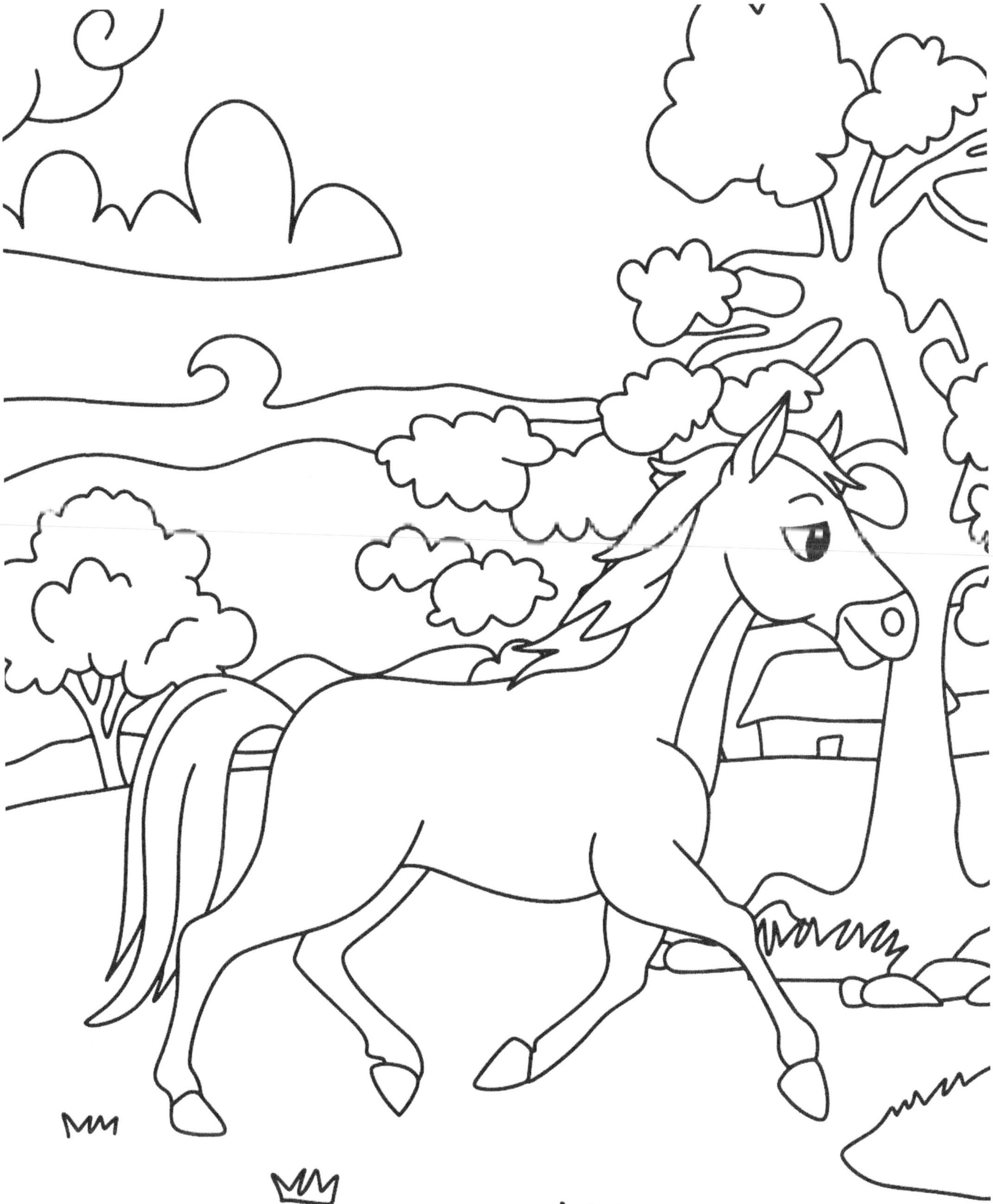

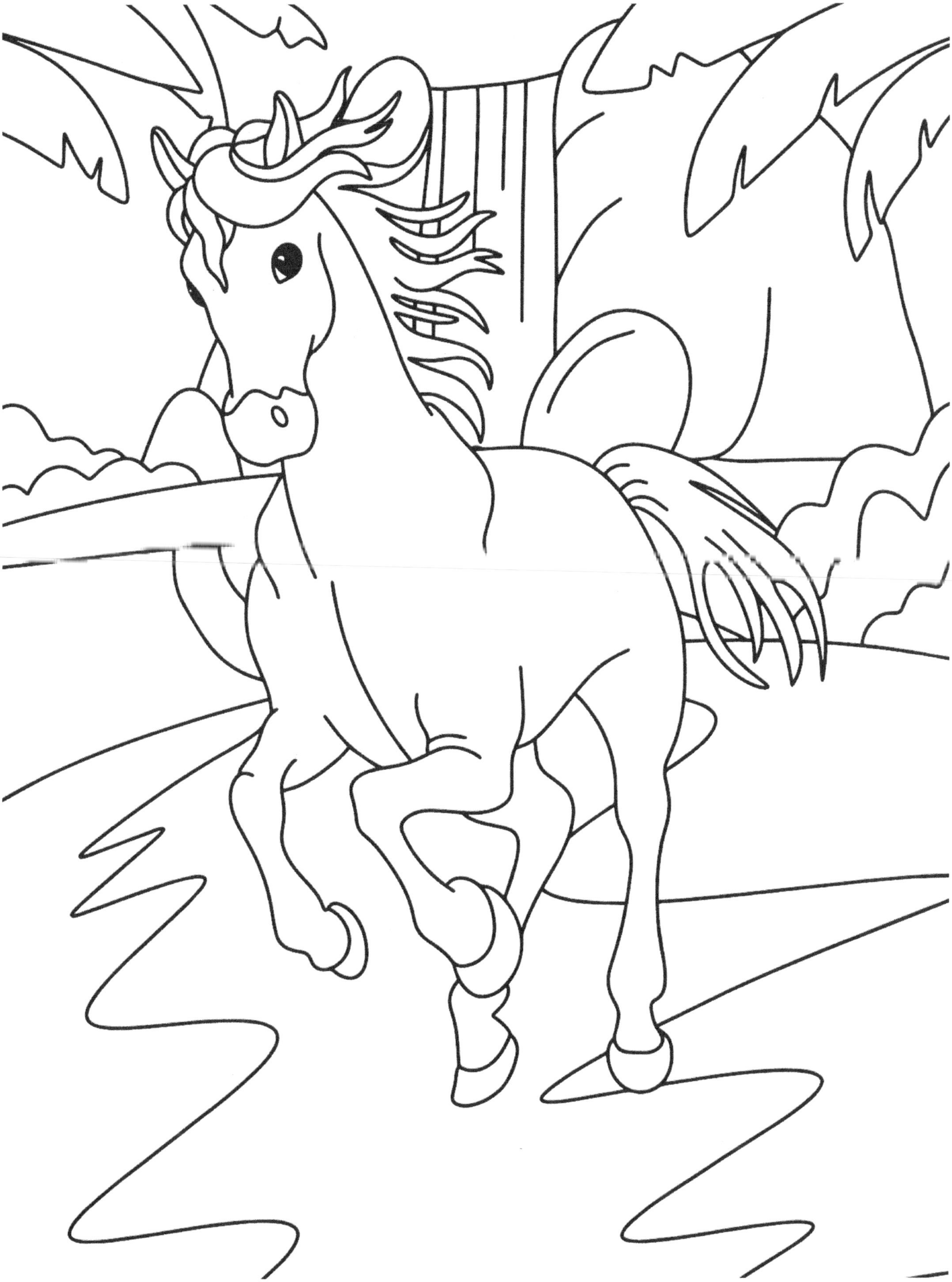

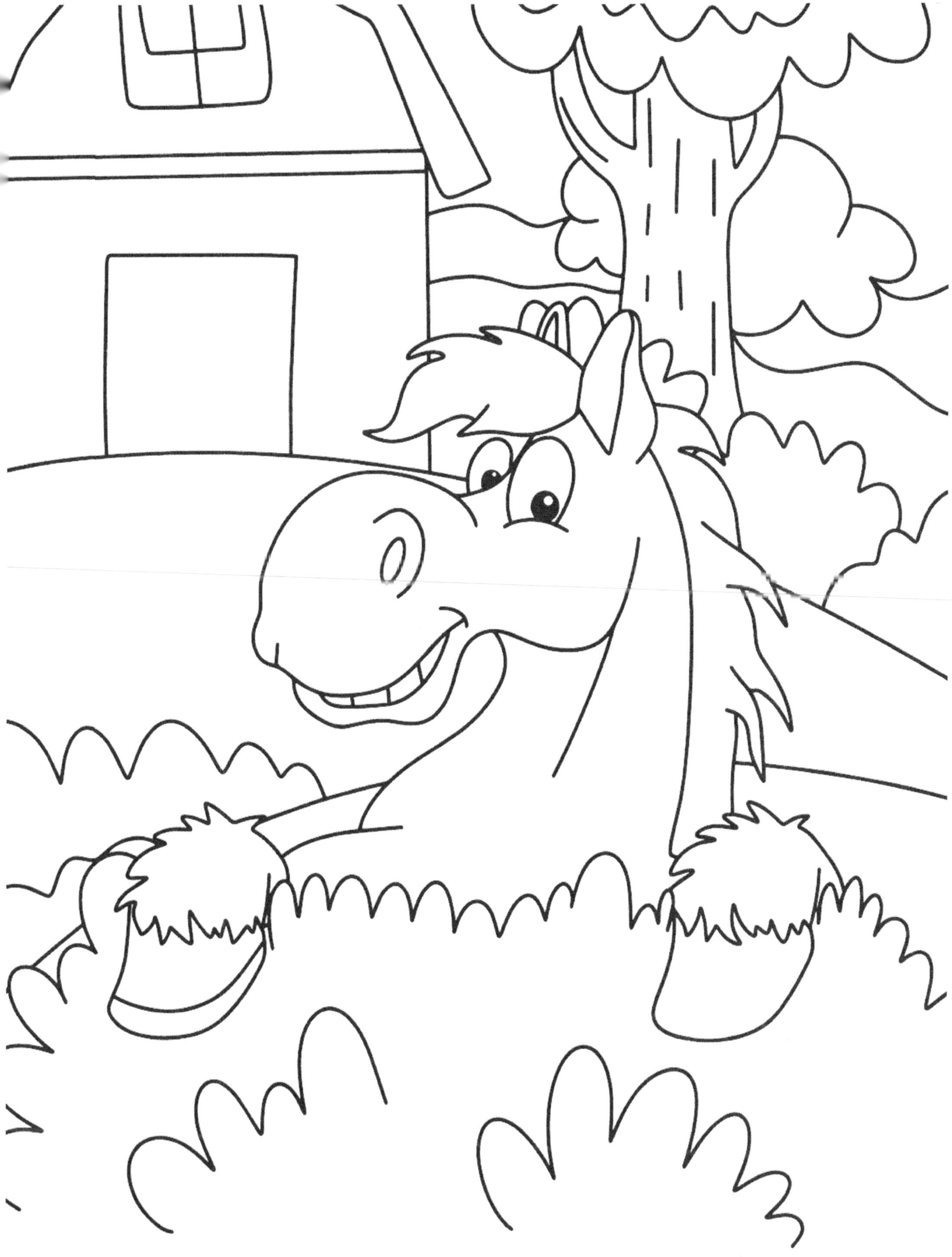

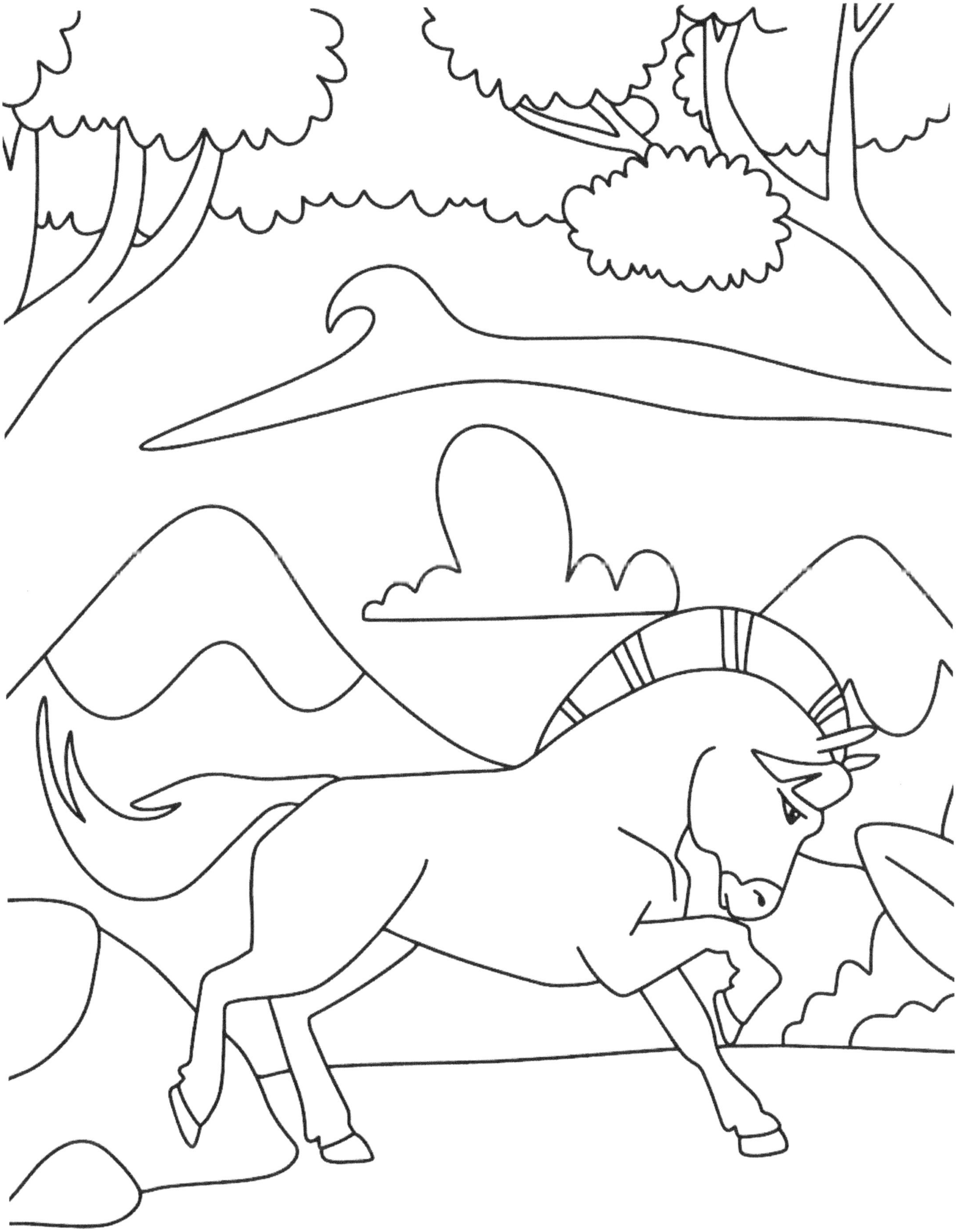

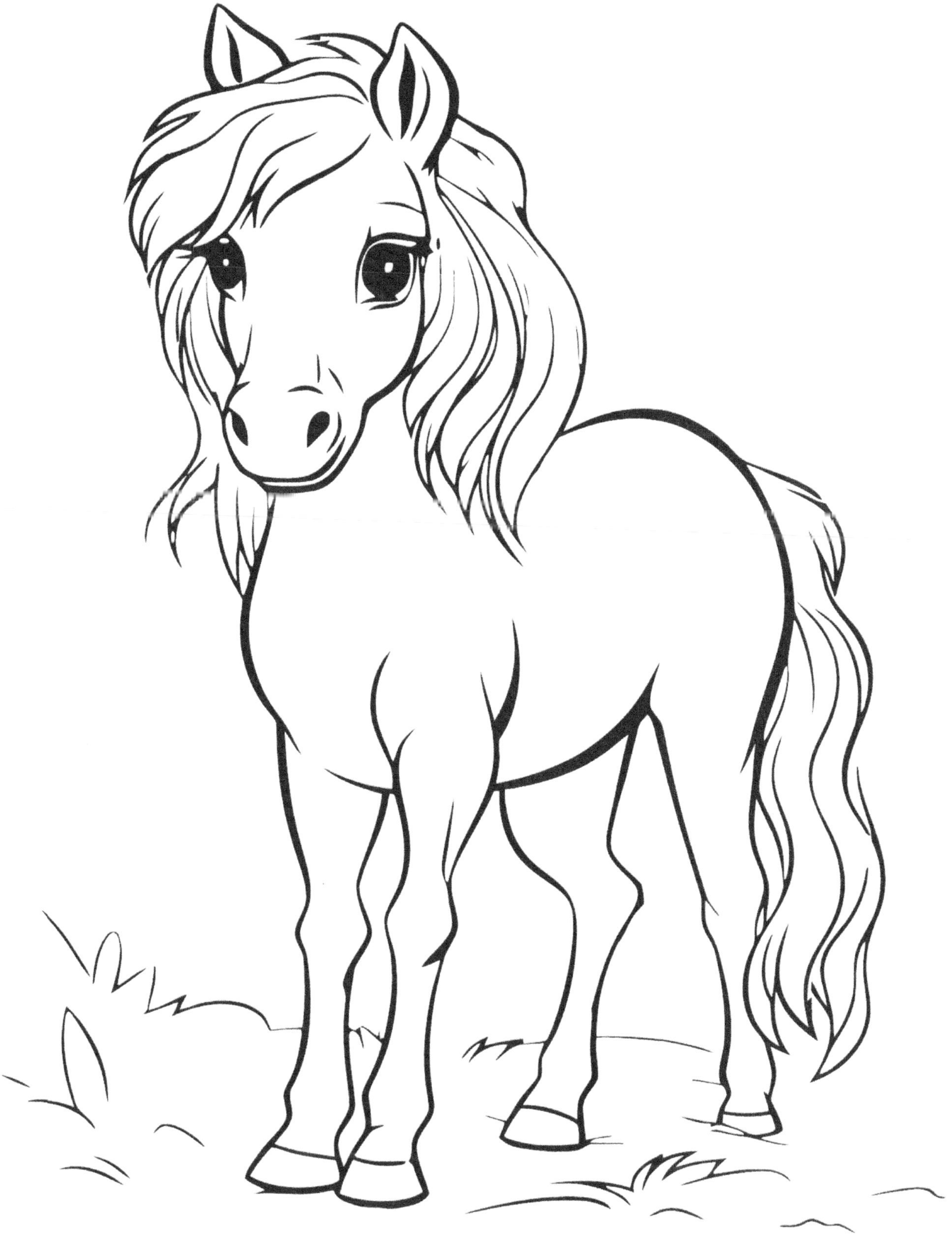

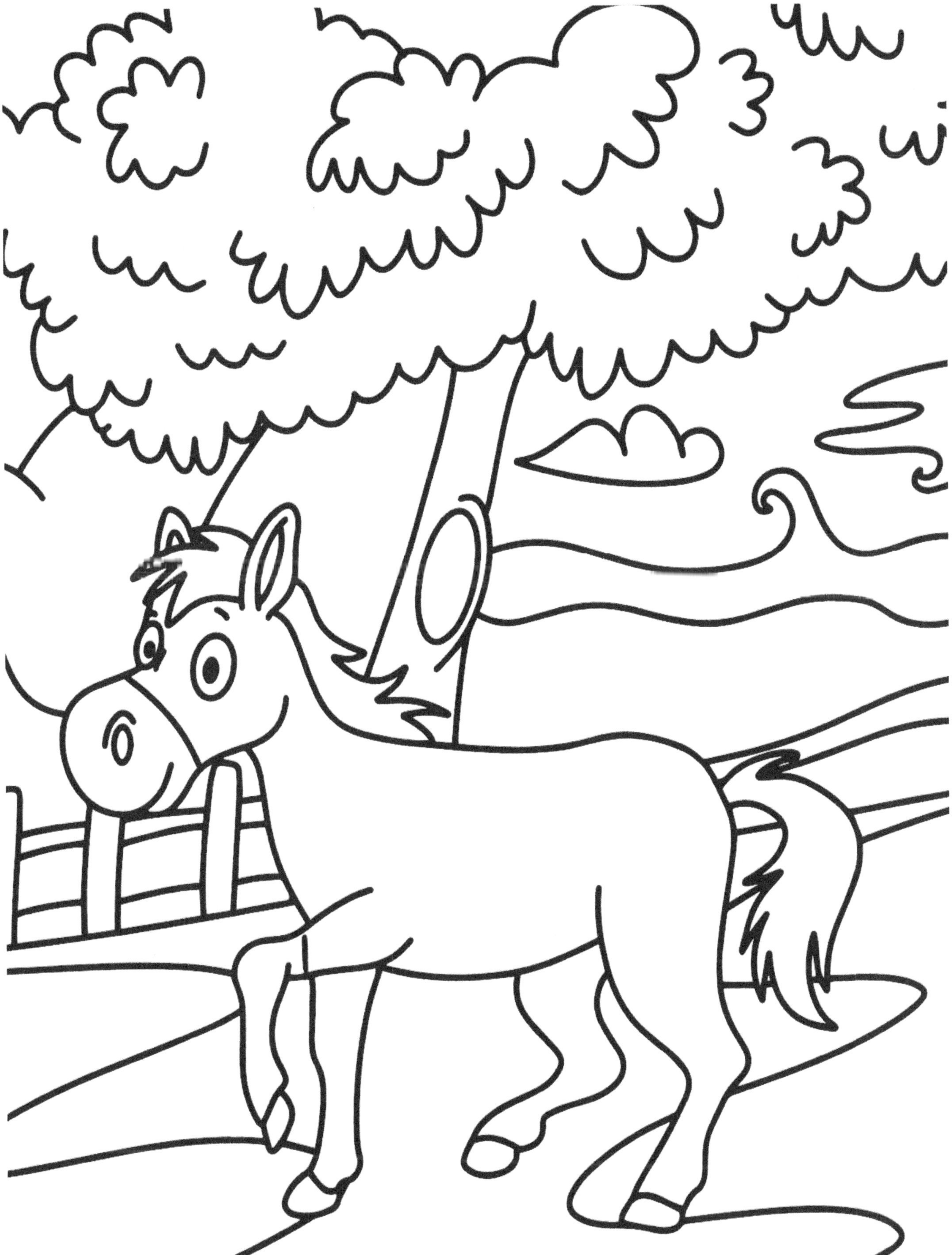

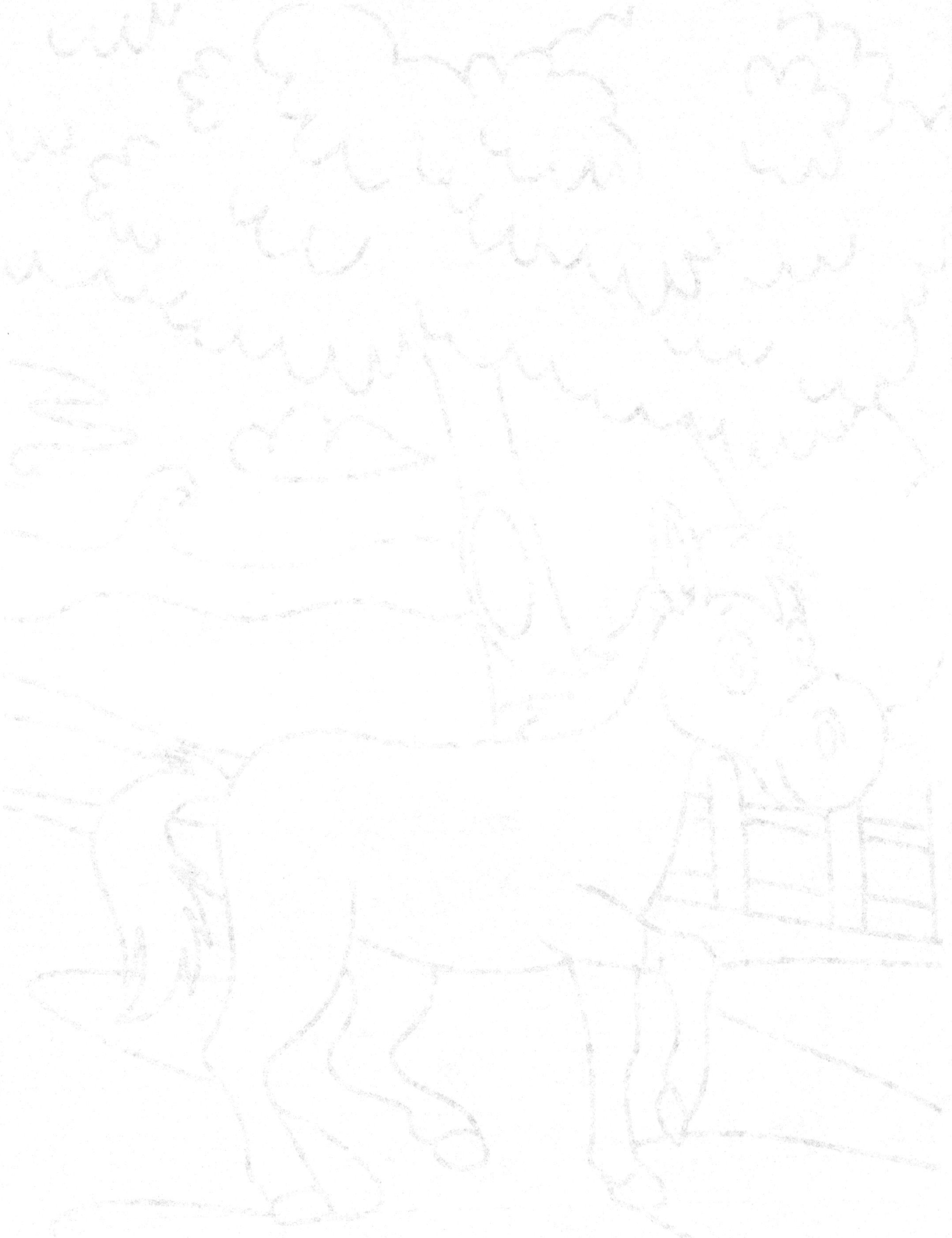

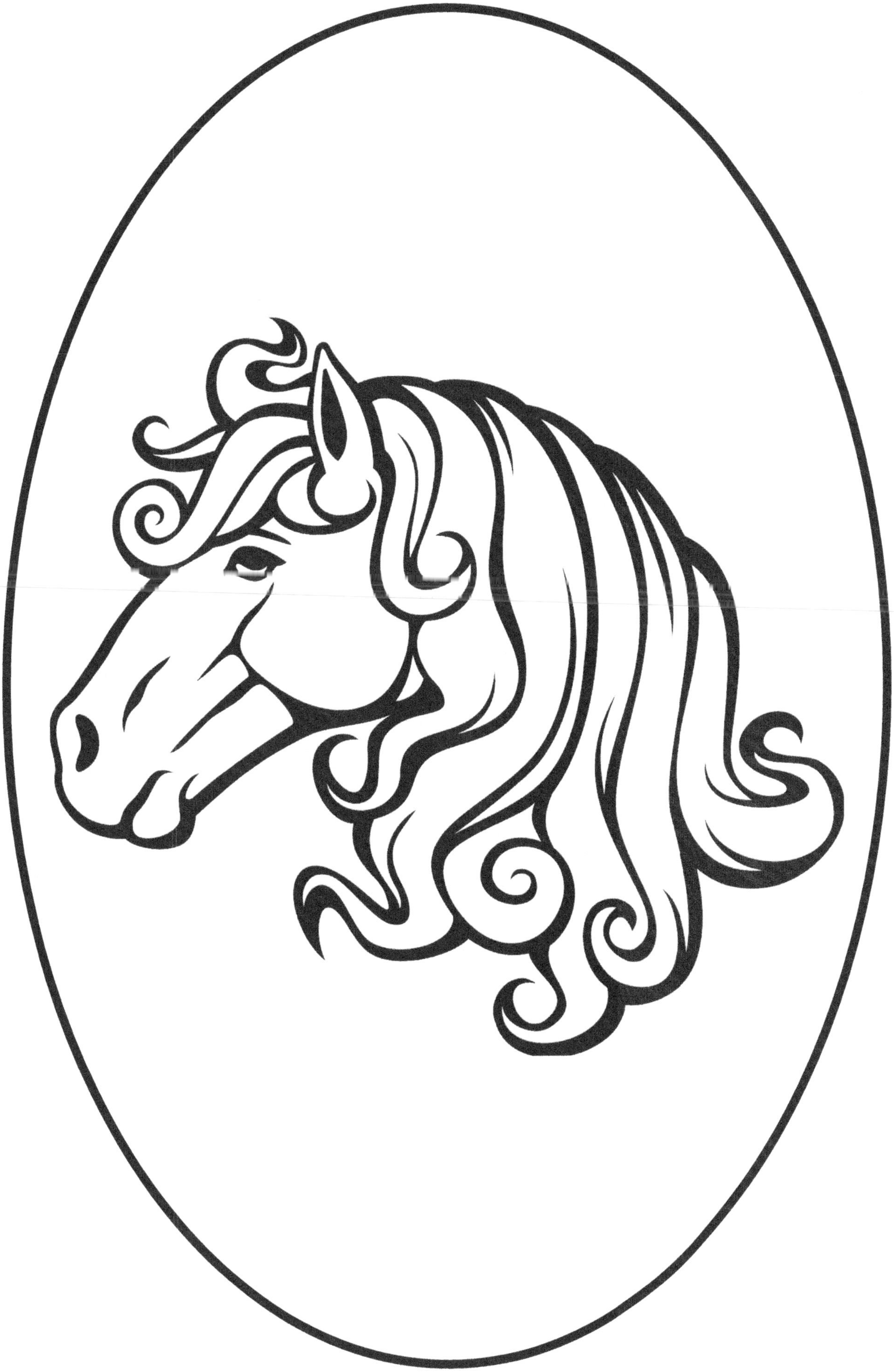

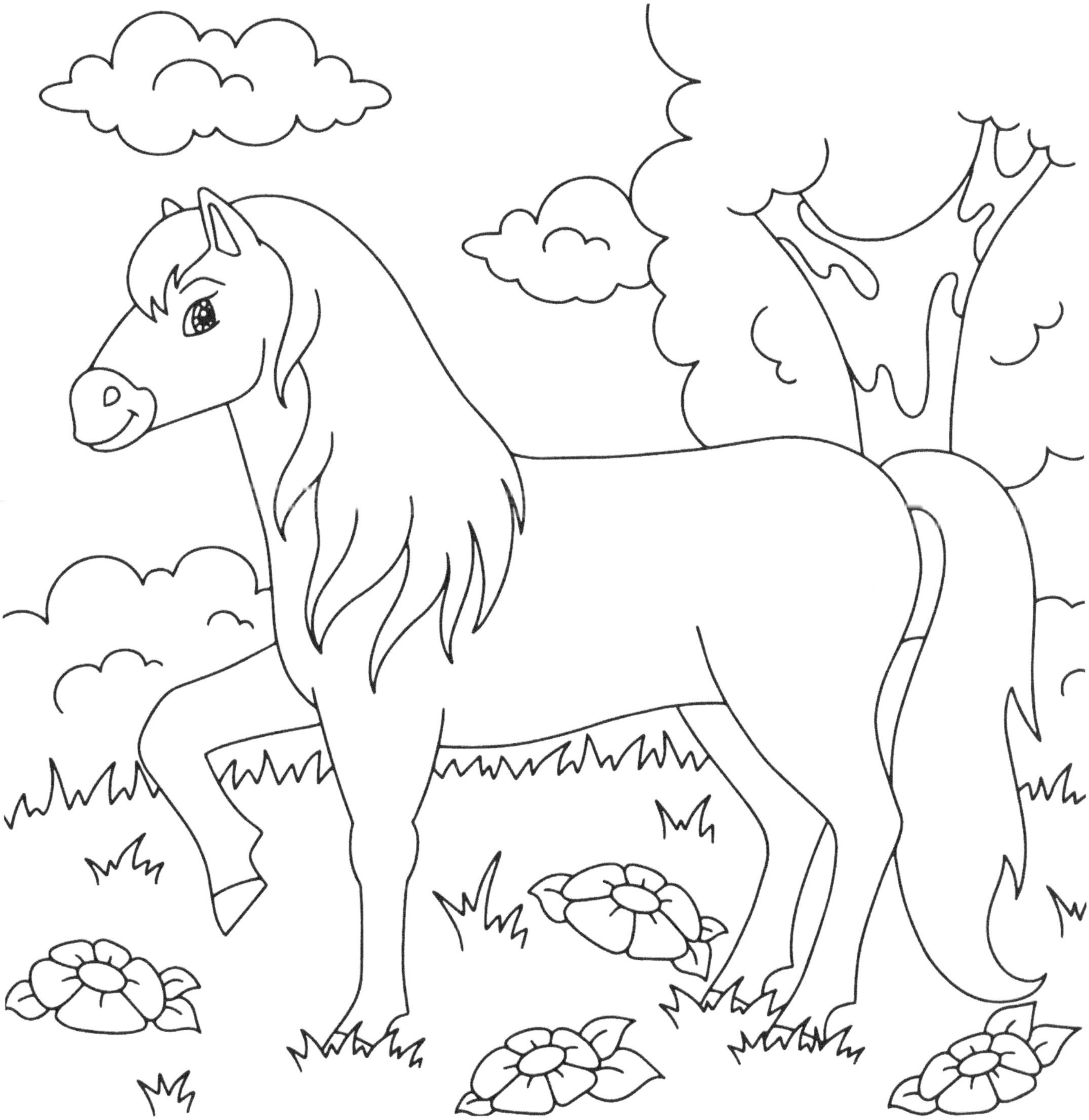

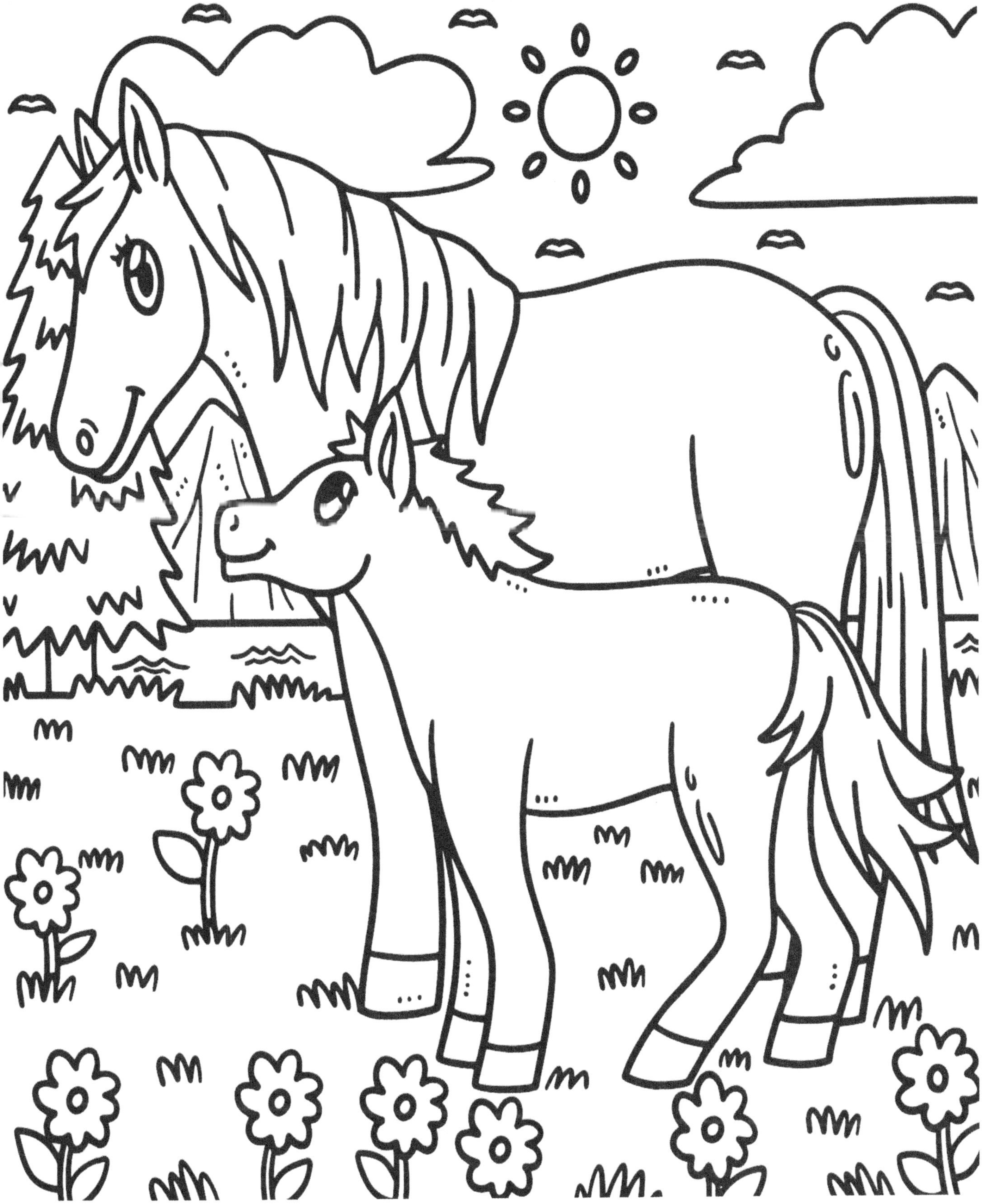

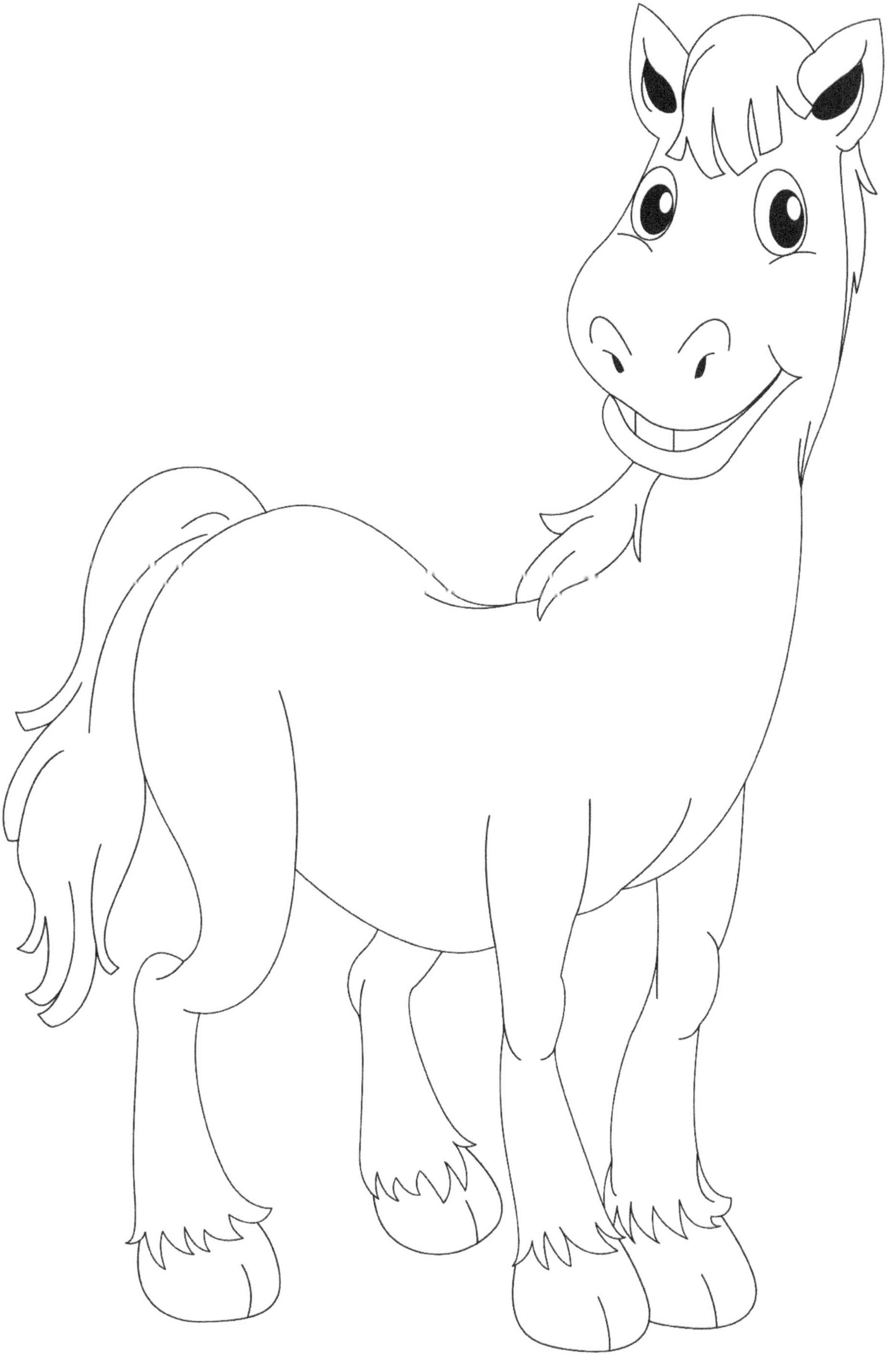

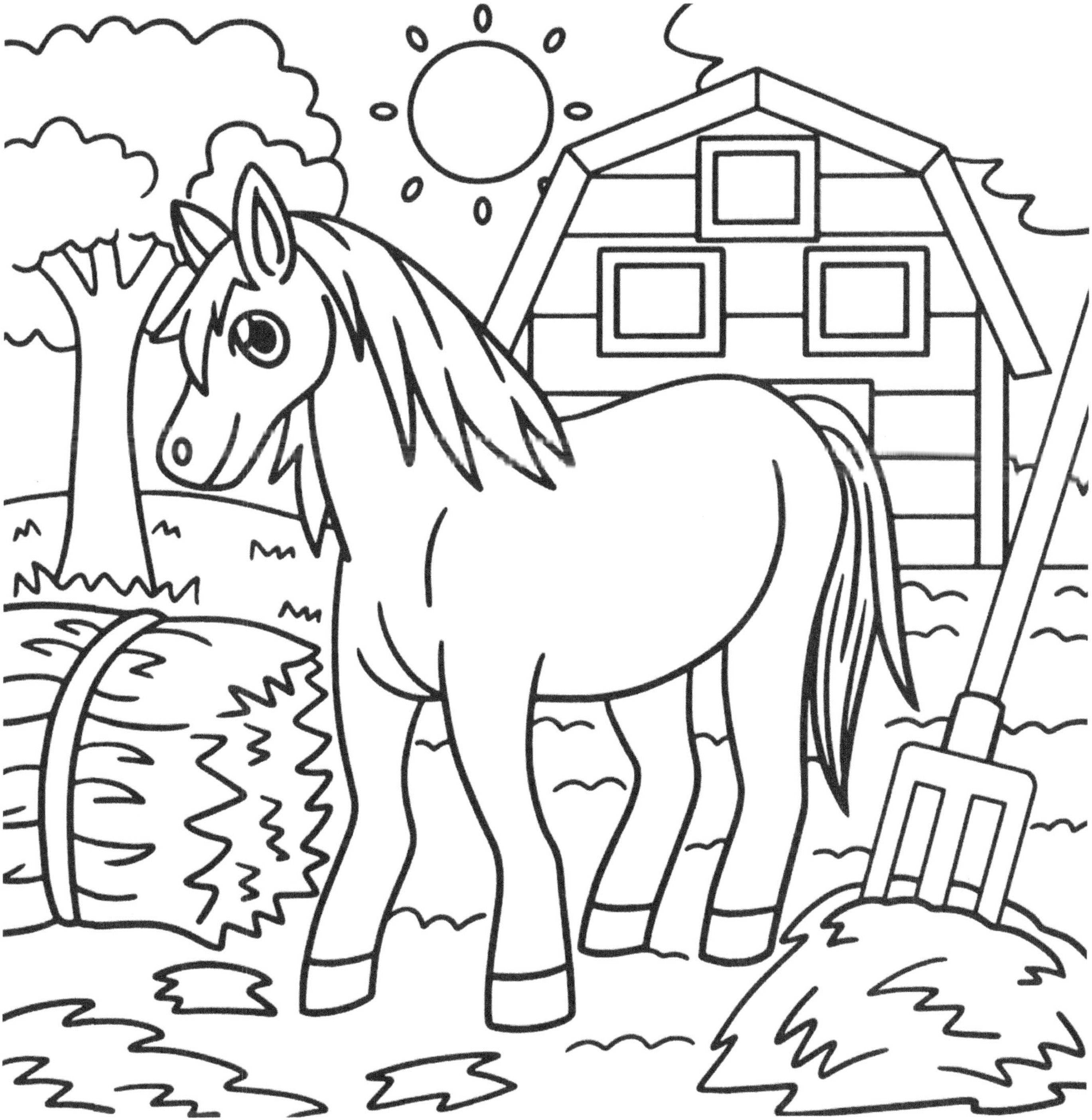

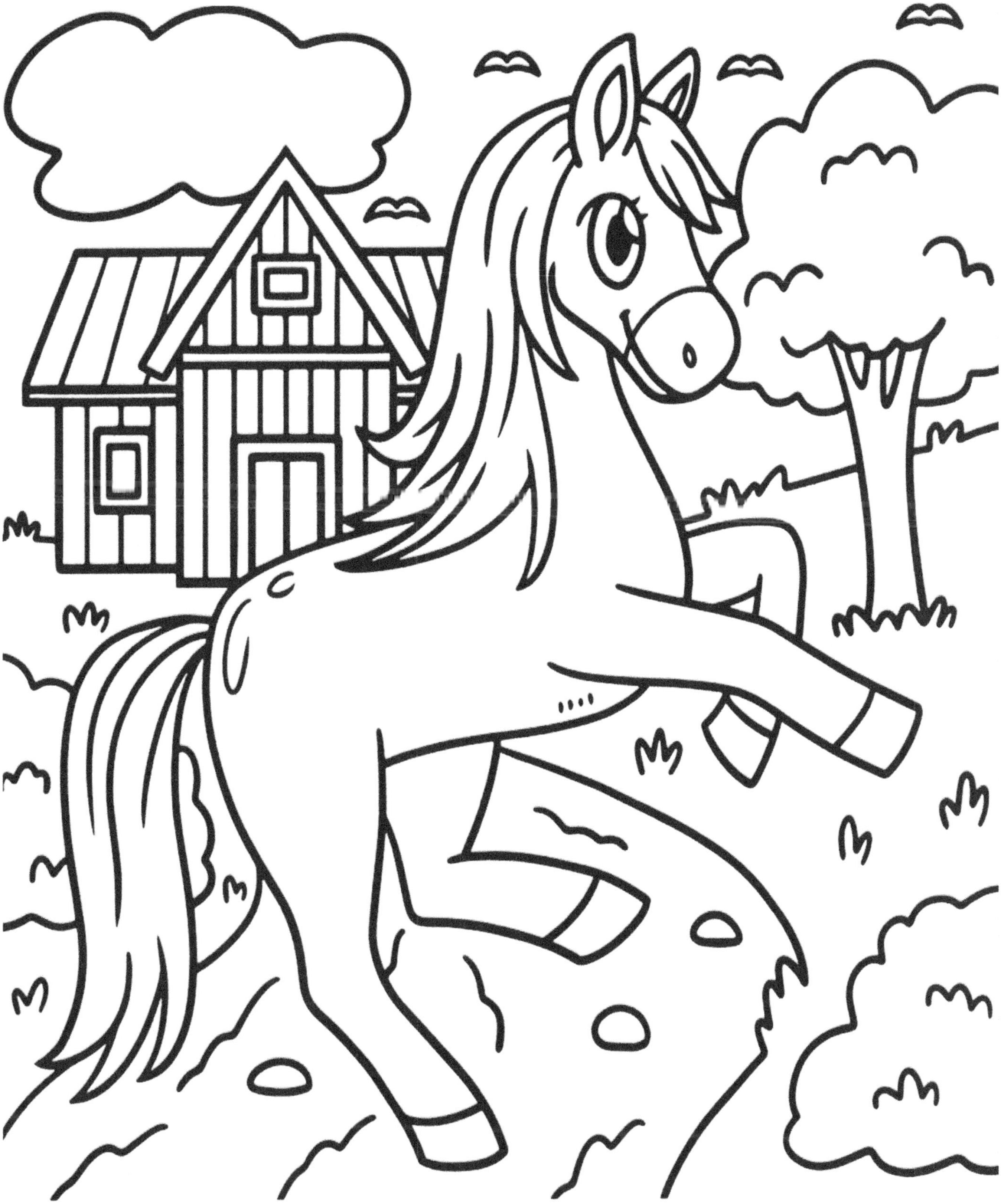

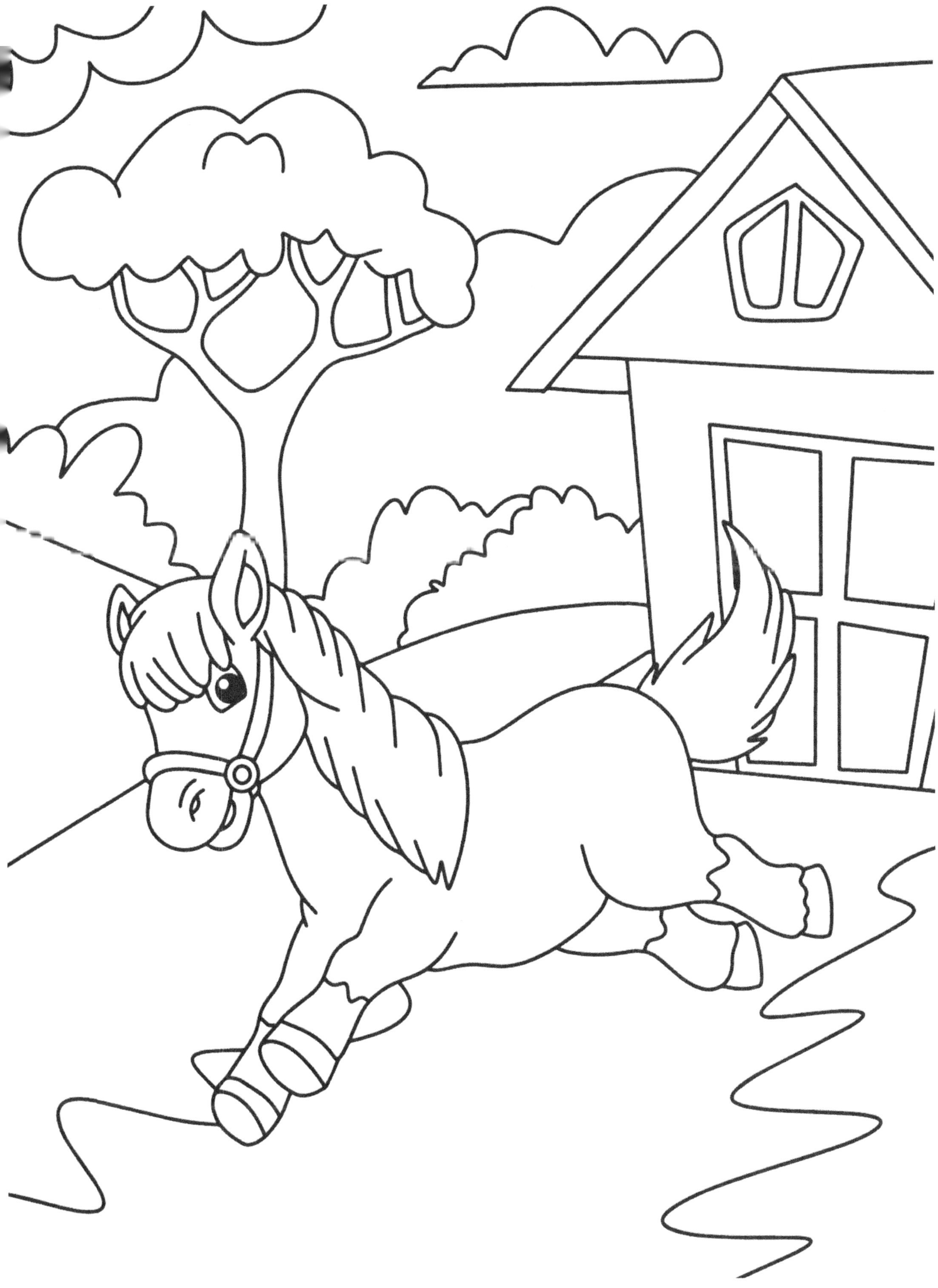

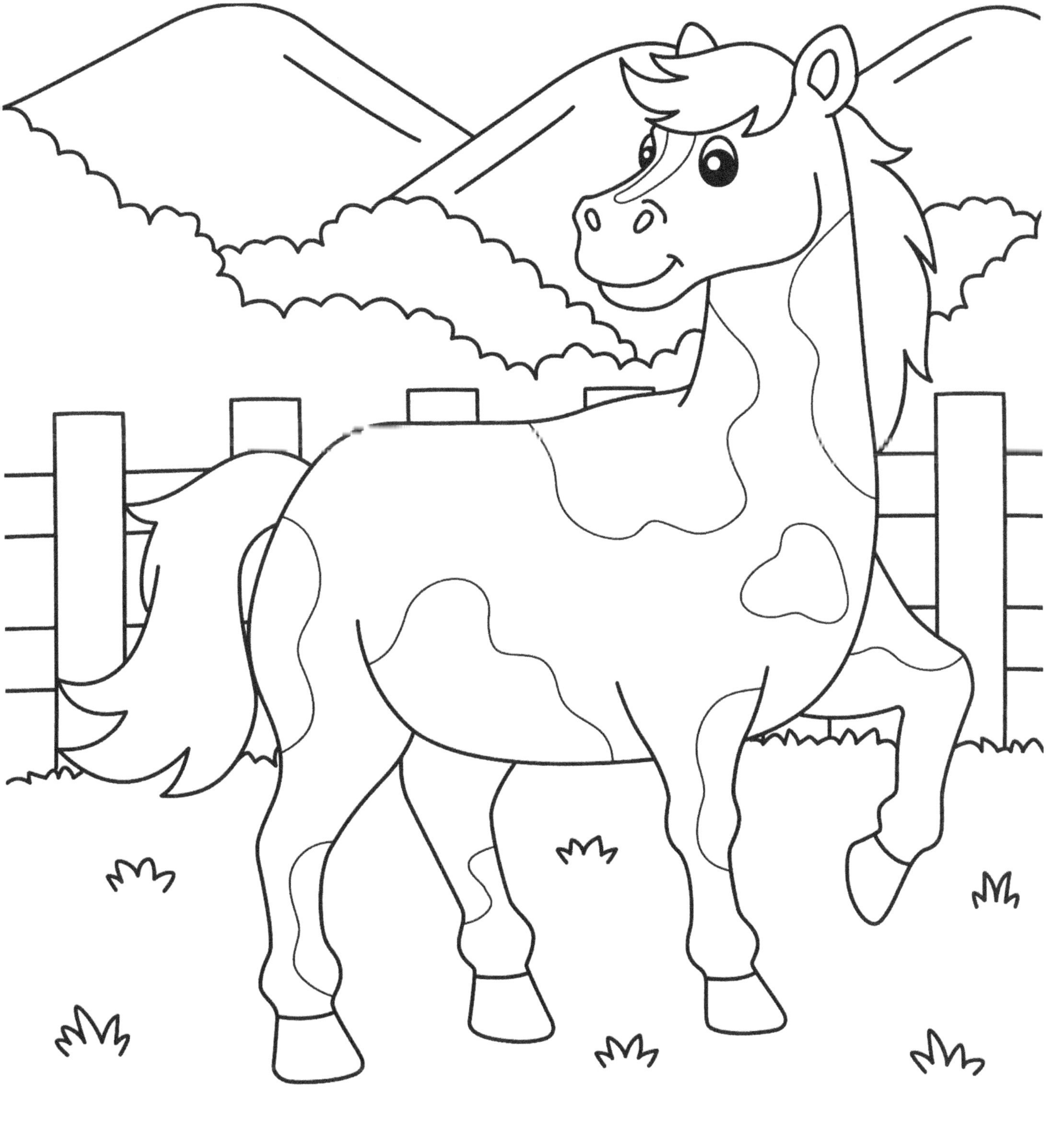

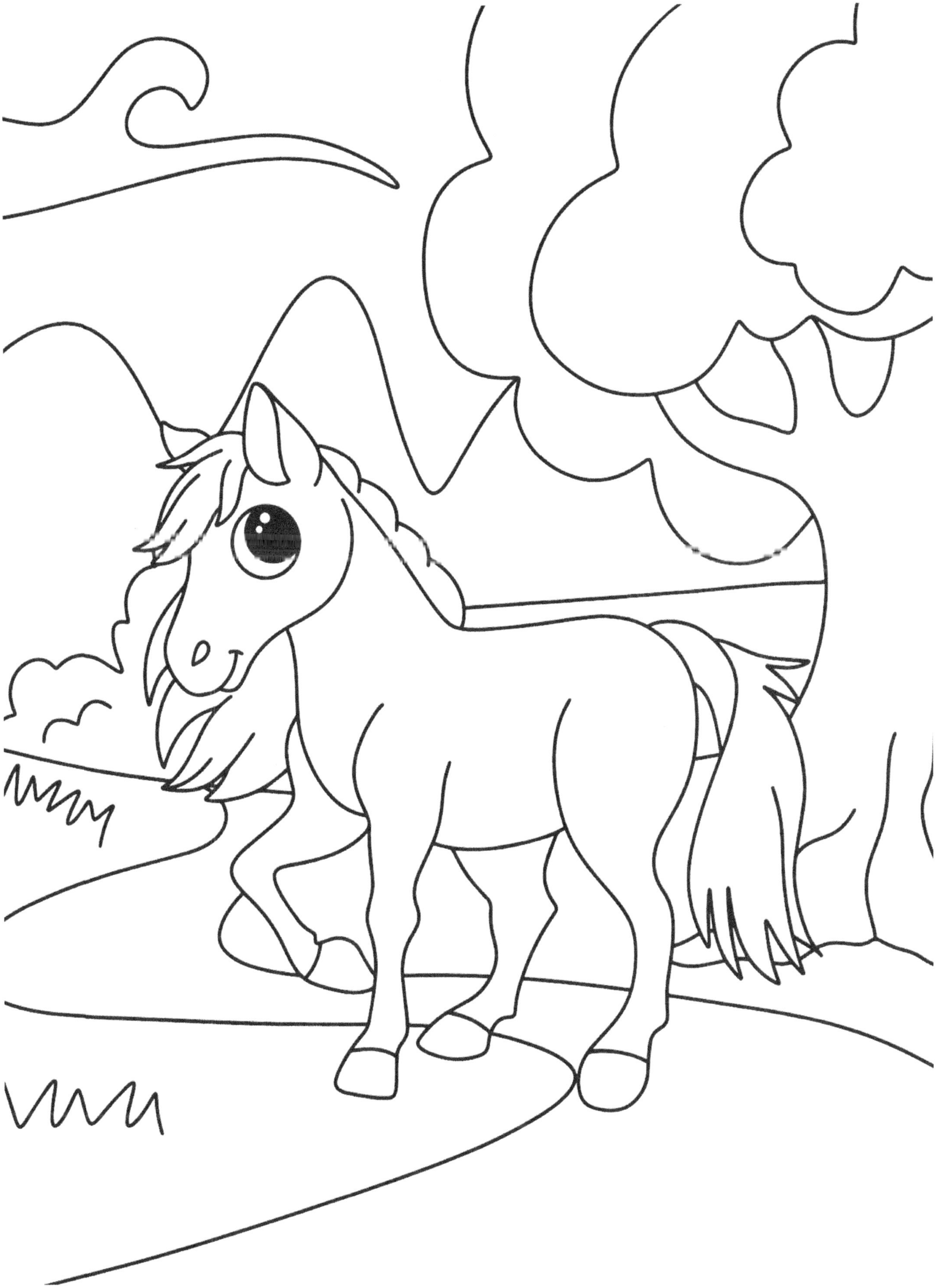

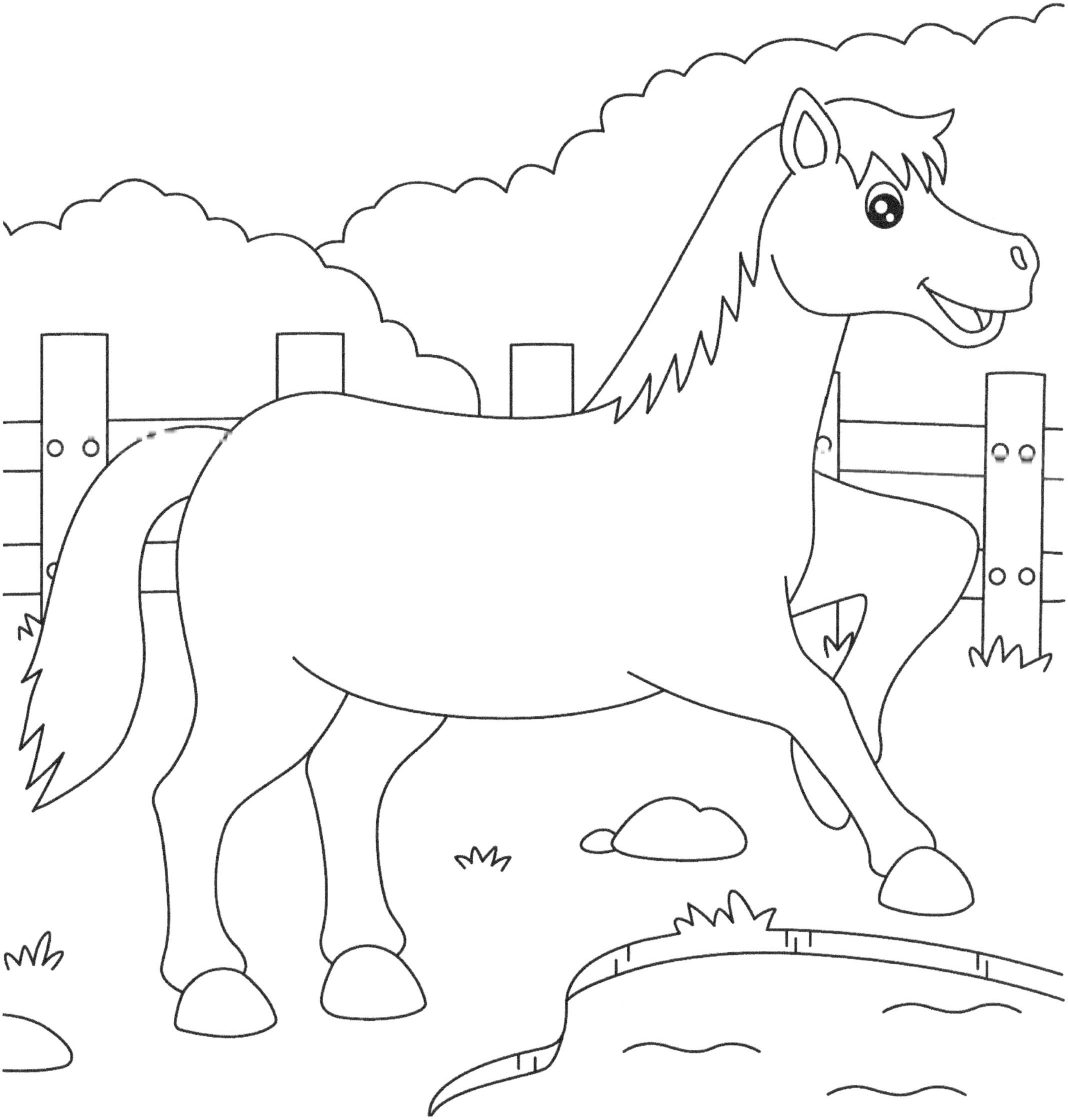

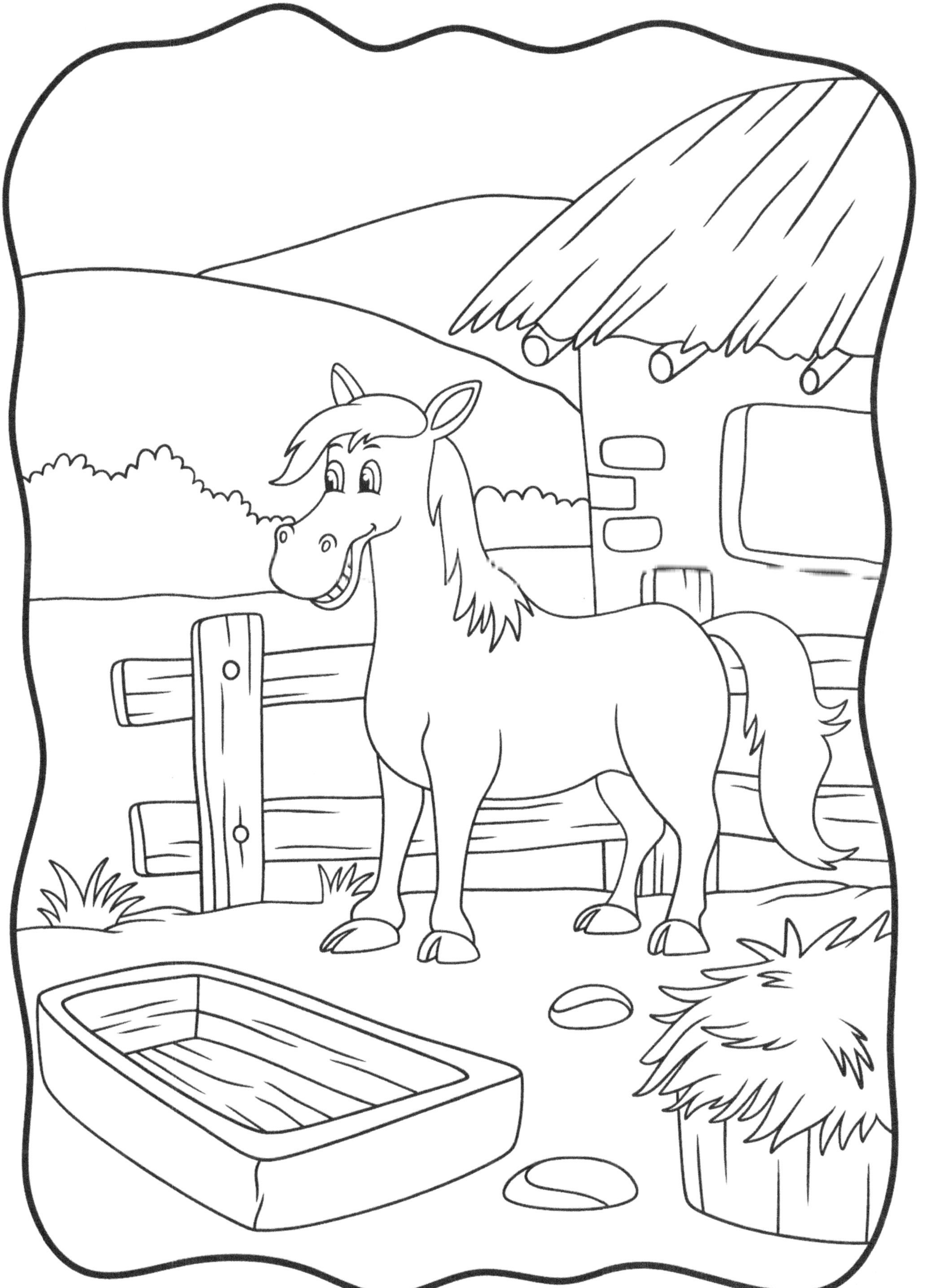

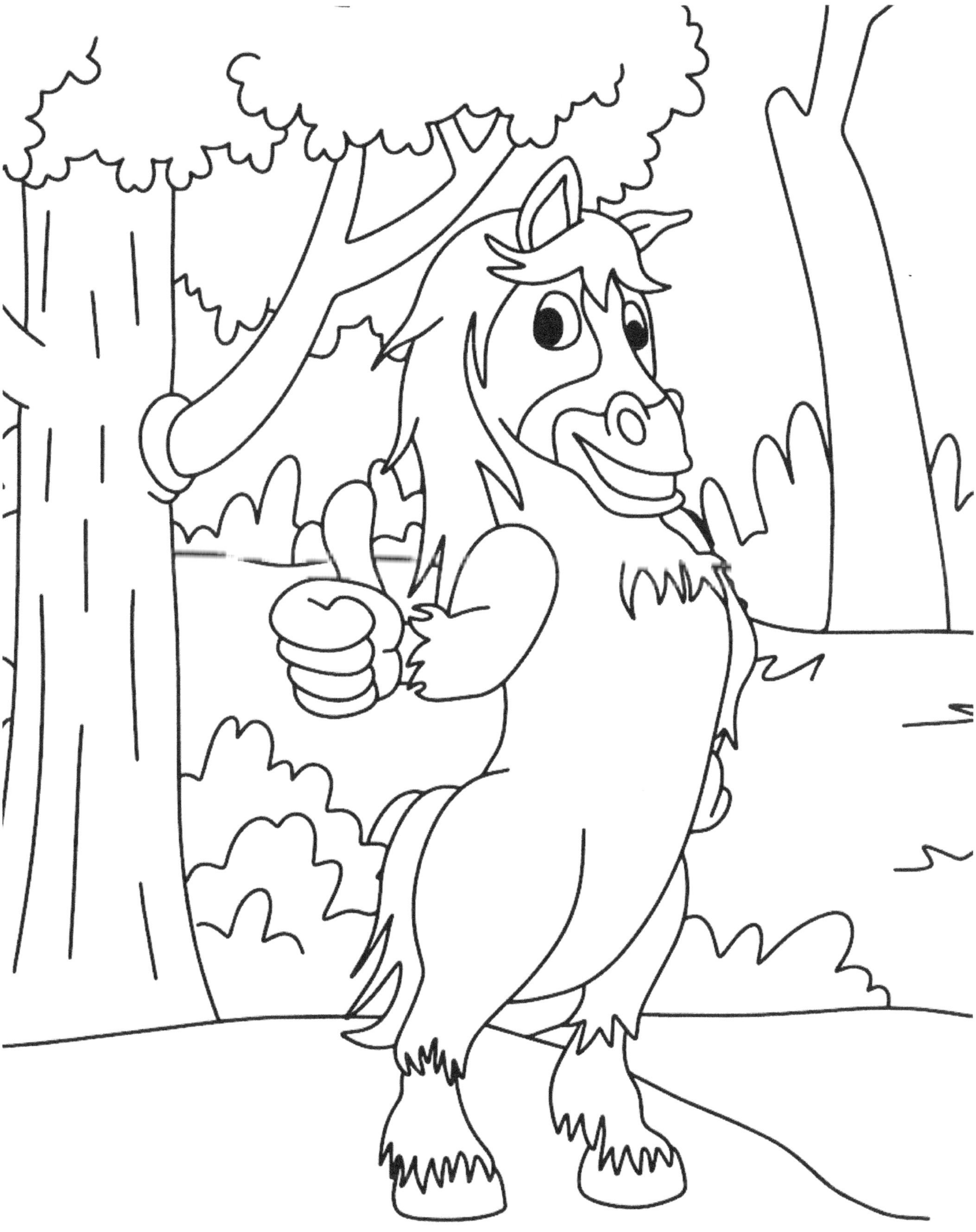

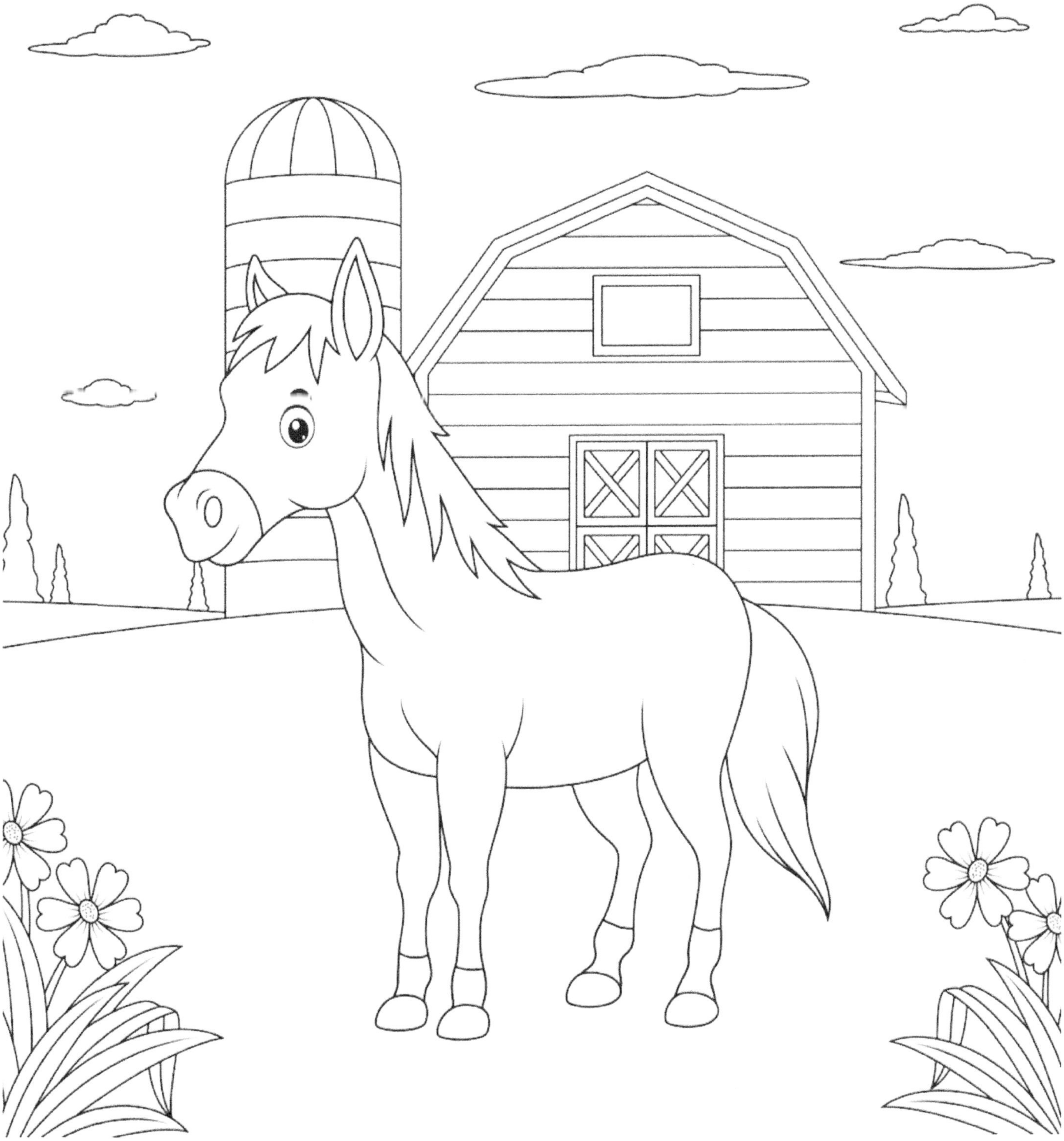

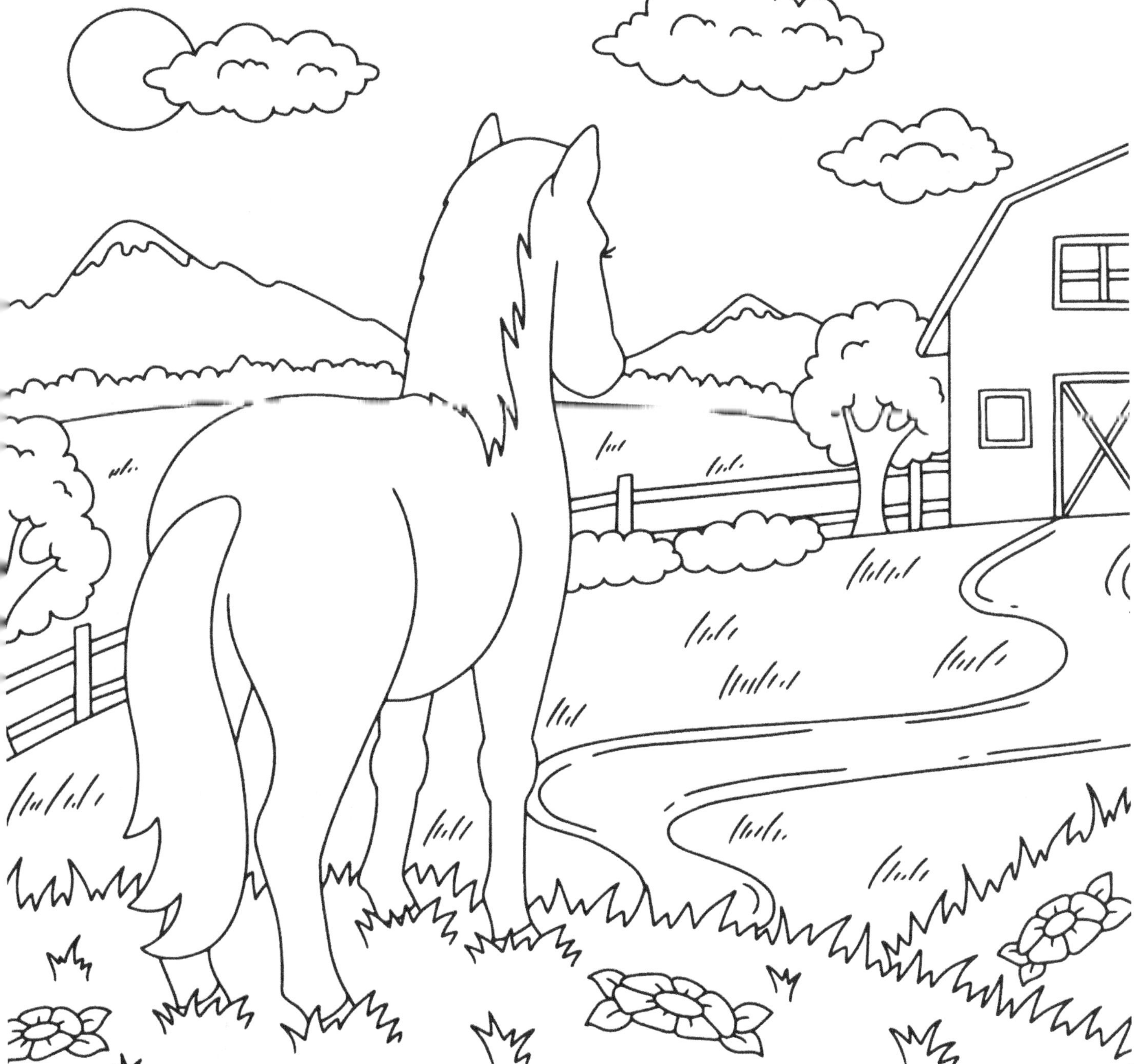

FOR AGES 3-8
TRUCKS
TRAINS
CARS
PLANES
COLORING BOOK

Made in the USA
Monee, IL
22 November 2023

47102376R00044